A
LOOSE
GRIP

A LOOSE GRIP

Governance in a Republic
"If you can keep it"
and
The Trump Thing

Howard Asher, Psy.D.

Uncommon Sense Press

(^_ ')

Los Angeles

Published by Uncommon Sense Press

Library of Congress Control Number: Pending

Publisher's Cataloging-In-Publication

Names:	Asher, Howard, author.
Title:	A loose grip : governance in a republic "if you can keep it" and the Trump thing / Howard Asher, Psy.D.
Description:	Los Angeles : Uncommon Sense Press, [2019]	Includes bibliographical references and index.
Identifiers:	ISBN: 978-1-7330020-0-4 (hardcover)	978-1-7330020-1-1 (paperback)	978-1-7330020-2-8 (eBook)	LCCN: 2019-XXXXXX
Subjects:	LCSH: United States--Politics and government--2017-	United States--Politics and government -21st century.	Trump, Donald, 1946-	United States--Politics and government --History.	Political culture--United States--Psychological aspects.	Politics and culture--United States--Psychological aspects.	Social structure--United States.	Popular culture-- United States--Psychological aspects.	Right and left (Political science)--United States-- Psychological aspects.	Conservatism--United States--History--21st century.	Polarization (Social sciences)--Political aspects--United States.	Political participation-- Moral and ethical aspects--United States.	Truthfulness and falsehood--Political aspects-- United States.	Opposition (Political science)--United States--Psychological aspects.	Communication in politics--Psychological aspects.	Corporate power--Political aspects--United States.	Branding (Marketing)--United States.
Classification:	LCC: E912 .A84 2019	DDC: 973.933--dc23

Book and Cover Design: Ghislain Viau of Creative Publishing Book Design

This is for my wife, an independent thinker
I love you

And our daughter and son, each independent thinkers
I love you both

Contents

Dear Reader,

A Loose Grip may be one of the most valuable reading experiences you have. It was written with that in mind. It's a book, so it's a compilation of printed words. There may be an occasional phrase, term, or word with which you are not familiar. Additionally, I flat out coined some of them. So I'm tipping you off here and now, there is a **glossary** to help you. It's a good read. It's organized by chapter and in order of appearance for easy reference. There are over one-hundred entries in the glossary, so I think I covered all you will need. Even if you know every word, it's more than a glossary it's a "history snack." *Check it out ...*

Here's another tip – read the book from cover to cover. It's worth it. The chapters are in a particular order to build sequentially the premises presented so that strong cohesion with the book's purpose is maintained. You can read chapters out of order if your interests are drawn to do so, but to get a full contextual comprehension, circle around to pick up the relevance of each chapter in its place. And of course, you can reread chapters or sections. But the point is to read the whole book through at least once.

I'm happy for what you are going to experience in the coming pages. Enjoy!

Best to You in All Good Things,

Howard

Introduction

BENJAMIN FRANKLIN WAS LEAVING INDEPENDENCE HALL on the last day of the Constitutional Convention of 1787 when a woman, maybe in the company of a group of people, approached him and asked, "Well, Dr. Franklin, what have we got, a republic or a monarchy?" Franklin's reply: "A republic, if you can keep it."

Notwithstanding the authenticity of this account, the profound meaning of it surpasses the necessity to verify its actual occurrence. Think about it – "If you can keep it." These might be the most important actionable five words expressed about what is at stake in our Republic.

Let's look at what each word means in the context of this Republic. "If" – means conditional and not certain. "You" – it's on you personally, you're accountable. "Can" – it's possible. "Keep" – hold on to, and as in keepsake, it's precious. "It" – well, that may be the biggest little word. What is "it?" Our Republic and much more.

This nation, this remarkable experiment … this Republic … can't and won't continue without its people's continuous development of virtue and wisdom. George Washington, John Adams,

Thomas Jefferson, and Benjamin Franklin said this about virtue. I added the part about wisdom. As has happened in other eras of our nation's history, we are at a fever pitch of polarization of ideology and misplaced, rabid, illegitimate hatred. We are in a crisis of understanding, or misunderstanding, with the real threat of losing what we need to "keep" if we are going to continue a trajectory of *life, liberty and the pursuit of happiness.*

I'm a psychotherapist with many years in the field. Treating patients involves helping them understand themselves and the world around them. Like a corrupt computer program, with "junk in" you get "junk out." The way you perceive and maneuver through and around any given social and political climate fundamentally activates functioning along a health-and-well-being/pathology-and-dysfunction continuum. Your understanding of, and your relationship with, society and its politics are determined by where you are on this continuum.

I don't want to get too psycho-theoretically wonky, but the developmental aspects of object relations theory offers an understanding of thought/emotional processes at work in an individual and extends into a group with social psychology dynamics that create a self-fulfilling echo chamber. If you have poor assumptions, without a validity check, the flaws in such assumptions magnify exponentially. Bad enough for the individual, but in a group the "junk" goes viral and the bad effects for everyone compound. "Junk in – junk out."

The point is, whether or not you like it, you have to get you're politics right. This doesn't mean join a particular political party. It means understanding *priorities* and *practicalities.* It also means understanding and identifying what I call "functional, or operational, truth." Functional truth is making decisions based on, let's say as an example, the earth is an irregular sphere turning on its axis. I realize this still

2

doesn't satisfy some people, but I'm going with it and I don't have the slightest problem doing so … and neither do you! Functional truth is the best state-of-the-art reality that reasonable understanding allows you to conclude for now. You go with it until something demonstrably compelling comes along to persuade you differently.

I wrote this book in such a way that you and I are having a conversation. Now, I realize in this format I'm doing all the talking. But feel free to "talk" to me as you read. Through this book, I'm sharing strong opinions, asking provocative questions, and offering serious advice. But I'm not lecturing. I'm talking with you, not at you. In essence, as you will see, this is a thought exercise … for you and me.

This book is divided into four parts. Part I, "A Republic and the Nature of People," lays out the foundations of our system of governance with a perspective on how and why it happened the way it did. The general public is woefully uneducated about any of this – a failure of our systems of education, as well as the lack of interest and curiosity by people in general about serious and relevant matters. My hope is to awaken interest through my narrative and to reveal the fascination and importance of this subject.

Part II, "The Trump Thing," takes on the current state of emotional turbulence (catharsis) and disruption embodied by the election of Donald Trump to the U.S. Presidency. Part II makes Part I all the more fascinating and relevant. If you stick with my assessments and analysis of the Trump Presidency, it's possible nobody gets hurt. You might even be better for it. At least that's my aim.

Part III, "Who's Crazy?," is an unavoidable topic for a book like this. There's a lot of crazy out there. It manifests in individuals and throughout the public at large on a huge scale. The book's title – *A Loose Grip* – has two meanings: (1) It refers to the uncertain hold we have on our Republic and the need to strengthen that grip, and (2) It refers to the precarious hold we have on our rationality and sanity as individuals and as a nation. *This means if we don't strengthen our grip the widespread irrationality and insanity present today will cause us to lose our Republic and ultimately our freedom.* Part III discusses these dangerous conditions, which are being deviously and effectively exploited in strategic and organized ways.

Part IV, "You," is a personalized reflection on the big philosophical orientations a person needs to work through continuously. As our Republic was established to form *a more perfect Union*, likewise, you should always be in the process of forming a more perfect (better) *you*. We, you, are the Republic. So, personal introspection is a part of *if you can keep it*.

Despite the formidable challenges of our times, this book lays out a positive perspective to be gained through greater understanding of all things related to our Republic and its continuance. There's a good chance you'll enjoy *A Loose Grip*. You may strengthen your conviction on how you see things or you may change what you think to maintain your intellectual integrity. We need wisdom, individually and collectively, to make it as a nation, as a republic.

Wisdom requires a quiet understanding of everything you encounter as it happens to you. Wisdom requires courageous honesty and the welcoming of free thought. Freedom of thought is a safeguard against flat earth, bloodletting, feudalism, and all conceptions that hinder our potential for growth and well-being.

Ronald Reagan said, "Freedom is never more than one generation away from extinction." Freedom carries the burden of intellectual vigilance and courage. So, *a republic, if we can keep it*, is freedom. And this freedom can slip away if it's held in no more than *a loose grip*.

PART I

A REPUBLIC AND THE NATURE OF PEOPLE

WE NEED TO UNDERSTAND WHAT A REPUBLIC IS AND WHAT it is not. Most of us probably heard the word "republic" for the first time when we ritually recited the *Pledge of Allegiance* at the beginning of the school day. When I grew up, its recitation was automatic and intended to shape young minds. To be sure, this ritual was indoctrination.

There's nothing evil in the *Pledge*, but these days it does ignite controversy in some large segments of our society. The controversy calls to question or challenges the pride intended to be instilled by the *Pledge* into our psyche, reinforced by its routine recitation. Moreover, the *Pledge* helps promote the idea our nation, the United States of America, is an exceptional nation in the extreme positive.

Current movements in mainstream left-leaning politics all the way to fringe leftism sees this "exceptionalism" idea as arrogant, egotistical, and embarrassing. Some would go so far as to say it's jingoistic and dangerous. The well-entrenched climate and administration of "political correctness" fosters and nourishes this view.

The problem though, if an unbiased, honest, and accurate assessment concludes that this nation *is* exceptional based on discernible measures, is why shouldn't this be acknowledged? Moreover, it *must* be acknowledged so the positive effects of this exceptionalism can continue and even improve. If a medicine is discovered that helps or cures a disease where other treatments were less effective, it's absurd not to recognize and be grateful for the superiority of this medicine.

"… and to the Republic for which it stands …" One day, for no apparent reason that I was aware, my fourth grade teacher, Mrs. Green, abruptly interrupted our usual drone-like recitation of the *Pledge* to ask, "Do you kids know the meaning of what you're saying?" Of course we didn't! What followed was my first breakdown and analysis of the *Pledge* via Mrs. Green's guidance of the discussion. She was a very good teacher. I still didn't really understand the *Pledge*, but I got the idea it was much layered with serious principles. A republic is one of those principles.

A republic is a form of governance in which ultimate authority rests in the people to elect those among them to govern the affairs of their society on behalf of the electorate and the citizen body. It is representative government.

The word *republic* comes from the Latin word *respublica,* which loosely means "public affairs" or "matters." In a republic there is no monarch or royal sovereign. In a republic all governing officials, including the head of state, are elected by the citizenry. No one inherits any office or head of state through birthright.

Our founders came from a monarchy; they were well-studied in the great philosophers (Cicero, Locke, Montesquieu, Rousseau, and others) and educated on the great civilizations in history. With their combined comprehensive knowledge, understanding, and sensibilities they resolved, hoping for the better, to establish a republic.

If you can keep it… I don't know of any more suitable words, cautionary and prophetic, that apply to the essence of our job as citizens of this nation. I'm definitely brainwashed about how special and valuable "the experiment" is. My sense about the exceptionalism of this nation *is* hardwired into my psyche. But education, experience, and critical thinking have added to my understanding and world view. Beyond my youthful exposure to iconic ideas and the earliest influences of my formation as a person, adult sensibilities and sophistication eventually took hold. And as a thoughtful adult, I *know* this is an *exceptional* nation. And I *know* keeping what we have as a republic on our way toward *a more perfect Union* has always been a struggle very close to breaking.

From the Industrial Revolution to the Whisky Rebellion to the Alien and Sedition Acts to the War of 1812 to the trail of tears to bloody Kansas to the Civil War to World War I to women's suffrage to the Great Depression to World War II to the Cold War to the Civil Rights movement to the Vietnam War to 9/11 to the epidemics of drug addiction, homelessness, ignorance, complacency, apathy, to perpetual political polarization, and not to go unmentioned, the assassination of four presidents as well as a number of assassination attempts on presidents, holding on to the republic has been a continuous endeavor and challenge. As Billy

Joel wrote, "We didn't start the fire. It was always burning since the world's been turning."

America is a *democratic republic*. That's the best shorthand description of this nation's system of governance. It's not a pure democracy in which all the people decide everything all the time. A pure democracy would be chaotic, inefficient, and highly dysfunctional; it wouldn't be workable. A republic is representative government. Fellow citizens represent the people's interests throughout that republic. The representatives are elected democratically in a routine cycle of elections.

There was much debate among the founders about the kind of government the nation should have. Thomas Jefferson, for example, was in favor of more direct popular control, more democratic hands-on involvement. Jefferson also argued for Constitutional revision on a regular basis. James Madison disagreed, counter arguing that with regular changes reliability and durability of the Constitutional system would be weakened.

The founders were generally apprehensive about a democracy, believing mercurial public passions cause bad and frequent changes in policy. Hence, our Republic is not designed for rapid movement and efficiency. Our Republic is designed to enact law and policy only after thoughtful consideration, with a long duration of commitment, care, and procedural requirements. There are numerous checkpoints and procedures to navigate before any law and policy, desired by any faction, is enacted. This lengthy process avoids rash and impulsive action. Additionally, our Republic requires such law or policy be in accordance with the provisions of the *Constitution*.

Any change to the *Constitution* requires an amendment. Our Republic expects and respects the inevitability of opposition and controversy to any change in law and policy. The amendment process is specified in Article V of the *Constitution*. You probably know there are twenty-seven amendments to the *Constitution*, which includes the first ten amendments known as the *Bill of Rights*. You probably don't know, at least I didn't until I did the research, there have been over 11,600 proposed amendments. This certainly demonstrates the *Constitution* has proven to be stable and durable since it was ratified in 1789.

Every now and then someone comes along and adds clarification to principles that were established before their time. Abraham Lincoln did this with his closing words of his Gettysburg Address. If you swap the word "government," the word Lincoln used, for the word "republic," the answer to the question – what kind of republic? – is – a republic *of the people, by the people, for the people.*

There are many pieces to this Republic. But when you get down to it, the Republic, as laid out by the "supreme law of the land" – the *Constitution* – exists to secure, as the *Pledge of Allegiance* reminds us, "*liberty and justice for all.*"

CHAPTER 1

Governance
A Flawed Prospect

HONEY BEES LIVE IN A STRUCTURED SOCIETY IN THE community of their hive. They do it instinctively and naturally. There never was a time in all history that a group of bees held a convention to work out the order of "bee" things. The bees didn't establish a mission statement and they didn't formally divvy up the work load. But honey bee society works like a charm. They've got it nailed down for good. Humans, conversely, are a perpetual work in progress, particularly with how we run our societies. The core determinate in how a given sovereign human society is run is in who holds the power and authority to make governing decisions.

Governance in a society is anything that is done, how it's done, and who does the managing of the human affairs of that society. Throughout the ages, there have been many systems of governance. "… it has been said that democracy is the worst form of government except all those other forms that have been tried from time to time ...." Winston Churchill said that November 11, 1947. This statement really underscores how governing is a precarious thing.

For better or worse, America launched its democratic republic when George Washington was inaugurated as president April 30, 1789. There's a thoughtful article written by Joseph Stromberg identifying the real start of the American Republic as happening seven years later, when Washington published his *Farewell Address* September 19, 1796. By way of this address, Washington established the peaceful transfer of power from one living person to another – a precedence for a principle that exemplifies the strength of our Republic.

* * *

So you've got yourself a republic and you have some rules and you've elected some people to run things by playing by those rules. In actuality, however, it doesn't play out that way. What actually happens? Well, governance happens. A bunch of elected guys and gals do whatever they can get away with. Some of the things they do might even be good for you and society. Many other things, not so much.

Leonard Bernstein's musical *West Side Story* is a 1960 reboot of Shakespeare's *Romeo and Juliet*. Governance is a lot like Bernstein doing this reinterpretation of the Shakespeare classic. Governance is running things in contemporary times, based on timeless or established principles. Running things is not only subject to the rules, it's subject to the interpretations and stylings of those who are elected and appointed. *That's governance.*

For instance, President Thomas Jefferson got an offer he couldn't refuse. The offer wasn't from Vito Corleone, but from France. France was having a "fire sale" of the Louisiana Territory. Jefferson didn't have the Constitutional authority to buy the expansive real estate.

But through some *treaty-lingo-kabuki* he finagled the government's "debit card" and made the purchase anyway. *That's governance.* For good measure, Jefferson reasoned since he purchased the land it would be good to see what he actually bought. So, he got Congress to pay for a camping trip later known as the *Lewis and Clark Expedition. That's governance.*

Our Republic has three branches of government. One branch makes the laws, another branch enforces the laws, and the other branch interprets the laws. These branches are supposed to stay out of each other's business, but there is continuous conflict between and among the branches when a branch steps out of "their lane." In other words, it's a *separation of powers* subject to *checks and balances.* In reality it gets pretty messy, particularly when you factor in the personal strengths and weaknesses of elected officials and the Senate-confirmed judicial appointees of the chief executive. *That's governance.*

The branch that deals with interpretation of the law really walks a tightrope of legal/illegal, right/wrong, and practical/ridiculous, while legal/illegal is all they're supposed to do. This branch of government is devoted to nothing more than interpreting the "crap" out of everything. And too often they still don't get it right. *That's governance.*

As far as interpretation is concerned, President Bill Clinton put it ridiculously well: "It depends upon what the meaning of the word 'is'… is." Clinton showed all of us we simply are not going to live in a world where you can be certain about anything, even things you're certain about. *That's governance.*

All too frequently, the interpretations and stylings of officials goes way off the rails. Here is just one example from each of the three branches: poll tax laws, wage and price controls, the Dred Scott

13

Decision. *That's governance.* (You can look these things up and see which branch did what.)

The point is our governance can do, and has done, awful things that hurt generations of Americans. But anarchy would have promised and still promises no better – only worse. No way around it, governance of some kind matters. In this Republic, our governance is the means as a society to bring about *a more perfect Union.*

CHAPTER 2

The Founding Principles
Just Ideas

THE AMERICAN REVOLUTION WAS MORE THAN A SMALL
group of governmental colonial elites taking risky and desperate
measures to break away from the mother country. These guys, these
trouble makers, who would later be called the Founding Fathers, took
great pains to justify their rebellion on moral grounds.

It wasn't enough for them to say, "we just want to run things our
way." There had to be a reason supported by morality and righteousness, underscored by critical thinking largely inspired by the ideas of
the Enlightenment. So Thomas Jefferson whipped-up the first draft
of the *Declaration of Independence*. He had some editing help from
a draft committee which included Benjamin Franklin, John Adams,
Roger Sherman, and Robert Livingston. To these guys of the colonial
congress, ideas mattered.

The big idea was *unalienable rights*. (*Side note:* Here's a factoid
– As it appears in the final parchment copies of the *Declaration of*

15

Independence there is some intrigue about the word "unalienable" as perhaps a misspelling, or printing error, or a purposeful spelling variation of "inalienable." In any case, both spellings mean the same thing: something you can't take away. If interested you can do your own research on the matter of the spelling.) So if you have an unalienable right and it's being violated, you have the moral authority to fight-off anyone or anything that's violating it. With regard to the American Revolution, that's your whole case in a nutshell for the rebellion … including a few more details such as *self-evident, created equal, life, liberty, and the pursuit of happiness*. Also, *taxation without representation* was big on their "do not like" list.

Once the American colonies dispensed with the matter of outlasting the then most formidable military force in the world and prevailing in the conflict to win independence, they had to turn to the question of "now what?" Britain, still reeling from the humiliation exacted by the "petulant children of the colonies," mockingly conveyed an attitude that was something like, *you broke it, you fix it … We did … and are continuing to do.*

Since the Founding Fathers were big on big ideas they had to build on what launched them to independence: the *Declaration of Independence*. They first tried to go with the *Articles of Confederation*, but it proved weak and ineffective for federal governance. Immediately after the War for Independence, the thirteen states were not really a cohesive nation. They were a confederation of states with no central authority to regulate currency, make trading agreements and treaties with other countries, provide for the common defense, or to wage war if it were necessary. The lack of centralized government posed a serious crisis. But the colonies had just fought a long bloody war to emancipate themselves from what they considered the tyranny of a distant central government. There was strong widespread sentiment that establishing a new central federal government would put the confederation of states right back where they were before the war, only with a new tyrant. The challenge, therefore, was to structure a government effective enough to govern federally while respecting and honoring state rights so states still enjoyed autonomy. A charter, a constitution, needed to be drawn-up that met the challenge, subject to the approval of the states.

The Constitutional Convention of 1787 was held in Philadelphia, Pennsylvania to take on the challenge of drawing-up a constitution. With the addition, four years later, of ten amendments known as the *Bill of Rights*, the delegates of the Constitutional Convention, the Founding Fathers, pulled it off. The *Constitution* was ratified by nine states and went into effect on March 4, 1789. On May 29, 1790 Rhode Island, the last of the thirteen states to do so, ratified what is now the oldest written constitution in operation in the world.

* * *

The *Constitution* laid out the structure of the federal government. It is representative government – a republic, democratically elected. There are three branches of government – Legislative, Executive, and Judicial – operating under the principle of *separation of powers*. This provides a system of *checks and balances*.

The *Bill of Rights* is a prohibition on specific governmental power. The government cannot establish a religion, cannot stop freedom of speech or freedom of the press, cannot stop peaceful assembling, and must allow for petitioning the government for grievances. The government can't infringe on the right to keep and bear arms. Unreasonable government intrusion into private affairs is prohibited without a warrant based on probable cause. You can't be compelled to be a witness against yourself, and are not subject to be tried for the same crime more than once; that is – no double jeopardy. Life, liberty, and property can't be taken from you without due process. Private property can't be taken for public use without proper compensation. An accused in a criminal prosecution has a right to a speedy public trail by an impartial jury. An accused can confront witnesses and have the assistance of counsel in their defense. The government can't impose excessive bail, fines, or inflict cruel and unusual punishment. There are rights that exist that can't be violated even though they are not explicitly mentioned in the *Constitution*. And, the stuff not addressed in the *Constitution* is left to the states and the people to work out.

* * *

The founders did something unique in history. They combined secular government and a society mostly oriented to religious values. They correctly considered Jewish foundation as related in the Old Testament critical to the basis for Christianity and the New Testament, and that they should be thought of together. In this way America is considered a secular government with Judeo-Christian foundational values. (The distinction between Judeo-Christian and Christian is noteworthy. America is the only country to define itself as Judeo-Christian. Other Western countries are historically Christian or secular today.)

America identified itself as having different values than the "old countries." It still does. European values are in equality, Muslim values are in theocracy, and Eastern values are in social conformity. Today in America, Judeo-Christian values are reflected in the inscriptions on American coins and what Dennis Prager calls "The American Trinity" – *In God We Trust, Liberty, E Pluribus Unum.*

* * *

18

One More Imperative Thing

The founders recognized that none of the principles and laws of governance laid out in the *Declaration of Independence*, the *Constitution*, and the *Bill of Rights* meant a damn thing if we Americans weren't generally good, decent people.

Benjamin Franklin said, "Only a virtuous people are capable of freedom. As nations become corrupt and vicious, they have more need of masters."

John Adams said, "… Our *Constitution* was made only for a moral and religious people. It is wholly inadequate to the government of any other."

Thomas Jefferson wrote, "Without virtue, happiness cannot be."

George Washington said, "Human rights can only be assured among a virtuous people. The general government . . . can never be in danger of degenerating into a monarchy, an oligarchy, an aristocracy, or any despotic or oppressive form so long as there is any virtue in the body of the people."

Yep, *a republic, if we can keep it.*

CHAPTER 3

Historical Perspective Always Keep It with You

IF YOU DON'T KNOW HISTORY, YOU WON'T GET THE JOKES. That's pretty important because good humor fishes out the ironies of the human condition, and that's where you get perspective … and a good laugh.

Without historical perspective you can't understand so many things about life, particularly societal/governmental dynamics related to the quality of living on a massive scale right down to you as an individual. It's necessary, therefore, to know, to understand, and to keep historical perspective as a constant backdrop of your awareness as a person. Moreover, your understanding needs to transcend common "bumper-sticker/fortune-cookie" simplicities about life. For example, I've come to dislike the pop-saying, "Those who don't know history are doomed to repeat it." There have been variations of this saying since these sentiments were originated; suffice it to say statesmen and others have said this or something like it. You can look it up.

I've come to dislike the saying because people who don't know much about history the way it should be understood pop-off this saying as if it's a "code phrase" giving access and membership into Mensa with all rights and privileges. As clever and profound as it may have seemed when I first heard it, I'm not sure it's even true. You see, there's the flip side to the coin. History is repeated precisely because tyrants and the elites *know* their history.

* * *

Throughout most of history, life has been awful for the general population and in many ways the privileged class as well. Life was so awful high infant mortality and short life spans were a blessing. Survival and an awful life were the preoccupation of living. In a different way, this preoccupation is still present today in classes of unhappy people. We'll get back to that in a bit.

When you see movies set in some historical period, there's an odd Hollywood peculiarity you may have noticed but shrugged off. In these movies, the teenage and adult characters or historical figures have teeth, perfect teeth. Hollywood, as it wants to do, makes concessions to our aesthetic sensitivities and gives us, for instance, William Wallace from *Braveheart* with Mel Gibson's attractive white smile. Now, did you ever see an ancient Greek or Roman bust with a grin or toothy smile? How about the Mona Lisa? Slight nuanced smile – yes; showing teeth – no. Portraits of the Founding Fathers – no teeth are seen. There is some controversy about this, but part of the explanation is throughout most of history people lost their teeth or their teeth were seriously rotted and crooked – very unattractive to say the least. I'm betting at the time the Scotsman Wallace was poking his finger in England's eye he didn't have the smile Mel Gibson has.

Dental care and hygiene as we know it today is a very recent phenomenon. We'll get back to that in a bit, too.

* * *

So, what does all this awful-living/dental-distress have to do with governance of a massive civil society? Well, just about everything. Let's pick-up the story of human existence after the fall of the Roman Empire in Christian Europe. This is where you see the human species has a collective survival mechanism that concocts state-of-the-art pragmatism. The population of Europe at this time was pretty screwed if they didn't come up with a successful enough societal civil system. What would be considered successful? If enough people could get by. And if the ones that didn't get by wouldn't complain too much. In other words, you just set the bar real low.

The first thing the people were told, and they sort of bought into it, was after you die that's where the good life is. This crap-life you're doing now, don't worry about it. Just behave yourself and you'll be rewarded when you're gone. That was a pretty hard sell, but the elites pulled it off because literacy was low. The elites, the church hierarchy, rigged the system by convincing the illiterate masses that salvation and the way to the good afterlife is brokered through the middle man, the local priest. The church even worked a scam for centuries to make money by selling indulgences, a sort of get out of purgatory/hell card. Eventually, Martin Luther was one of those who blew the whistle on all this and caused a *reformation*. Maybe you heard about it?

So, the ruling elites pretty much got everyone to wait until they died to have a good life. *I know, the irony is stunning*. Then the elites said whatever crappy life you do have we'll (the ruling class, the lords, and such) take care of you. Just work your asses off, give us

23

everything you have, and we'll see to it, as best we can, that raiders don't come and rape your women and kill you. "Deal?" "Sure," the people said, "deal."

This arrangement, cynically put, was a pragmatic foundation, in its time, of Western civilization.

Magna Carta

The signing of the *Magna Carta* in 1215 was a notable step that in essence would be the basis for moving away from divine rule, absolute monarchy, and tyranny. For many centuries, it never came close to accomplishing such. But there was something in its literal meaning demarking an idea that over time thoughtful, influential people couldn't ignore.

The full name, *Magna Carta Librertatum*, Medieval Latin for "the Great Charter of Liberties," documented the rights people had that monarchs had to honor. Monarchs were no longer just accountable to themselves. They were also accountable to the people at large. Over centuries, this would become the righteous perspective that any person can have toward a monarch or head of state – *you're not the boss of me.*

The Move ... and the *Constitution* of the United States of America

About 150 years after the Western Hemisphere was discovered, there was a certain kind of European with personality characteristics that included an adventurous spirit, a willingness to take risks, and a desire for something better for himself and his family (if he had one). Such people made the dangerous journey across the Atlantic to make a new home. That move set into motion an arch toward governance allowing for the greatest improvement in quality of life and standard of living enjoyed by the largest number of people in history. In his December 1,1862 annual speech to Congress, Abraham Lincoln, in referring to this nation, said "… the last best hope on earth." The benefits of this nation reach beyond its borders.

From the feudalism of post Roman imperialism; to the attempt to impose accountability and restriction on monarchy, as prescribed by the *Magna Carta*; to the direct relationship doctrine of the Reformation; to the challenges to monarchy and church by the thinkers of the Enlightenment; to arguments made for egalitarian government espoused in Thomas Paine's *Common Sense*, the Thirteen Colonies of North America initiated a throw down to mother Britain and its king by way of the *Declaration of Independence*. Among many things said in the document, the signers made a big deal about rights that can neither be given nor taken away – *life, liberty and the pursuit of happiness*. That's a long way from life is awful and the best you can do is be a vassal (medieval slave) and die.

The opening words of the *Constitution* are remarkable for first identifying the voice of the *Constitution*, "We the People," and then getting down to the purpose of the document, "… to form a more perfect Union." Most notably, it doesn't say to form a perfect Union. The qualifier, "a more" is perhaps the most powerful statement of humble self-awareness, practicality, and reality-based intellectual maturity in the entire document.

Right off the top, the *Constitution* is saying we're not perfect. But it also says that through the *Constitution* we're trying to move in the direction of "perfect." So, "the experiment" is a work in progress. The *Constitution* embodies the rules of governance by which our march toward unattainable perfection is to be carried. There are even

Constitutional provisions to make rule changes if deemed necessary. But the process of "deeming" is no small procedure. Affecting change and enacting amendments is purposely challenging – to protect us from our impulsive nature.

* * *

Getting Back to Two Things

Thing 1: There are many classes in society distinguished by countless identifiers. Among these classes is the "grievance class." This class may align with other classes, but it's sole purpose is to voice grievances no matter what.

In the 1953 film *The Wild One* Marlon Brando plays Johnny Strabler, a leader of a rowdy motorcycle gang. The gang's name is the "Black Rebels Motorcycle Club." A young lady asks Johnny, who's got a lot of antisocial attitude, "What are you rebelling against?" Johnny responds, "Whaddaya got?" The grievance class functions the same as gang leader Johnny. "What's your grievance?" The grievance class answer: "Whaddaya got?" The grievance class is so consumed by their complaints of "dire societal wrongs," it appears far more important to them always to have problems to feed the need for complaints than to actually resolve problems. Moreover, it's as if they want to do away with the system that has the best chance of advancing improvements, maybe even many things they want.

What's unfortunate is there *are* many things that call for grievance. But the grievance class saturates the public discourse with anything and everything, with irrelevance and absurdity; the noise of it drowns out legitimate ways to address necessary issues. There are many good things and bad things about this nation. With the grievance class in mind, it makes me think about babies and bath water.

Thing 2: Dental health is more widely available and accessible to the population at large than ever. But it's just a small example of a bigger unseen and unnoticed phenomenon. Put simply, an average person today, in this country and in many places throughout the world, lives much better than an upper-class, very wealthy person lived only a hundred years ago. Transportation, communication, education, residential housing, indoor climate control, entertainment, medical/dental care, and so on are vastly improved and enjoyed by most everyone today. All of the wealth that wealthy people had a hundred years ago couldn't buy what the average guy, or even a poor person, can get today. That's what this nation of people has done.

Perspective

So, let's not mince words. We have a nation founded on principles that, best case, we may aspire to, or worst case, we really don't understand or care about. America has always been, and continues to be, loaded with fault and injustice. And yet, as previously noted, because of this nation, the quality and standard of life have exponentially been affected in the positive not only for the greatest number of people in America, but throughout the world – like never before.

And so, before we and the grievance class go trashing the system and the generations of people who brought the advances that changed our lives for the better, we need to maintain the fundamentals (the *Constitution*) to continue forming *a more perfect Union,* as we are *the last best hope on earth… if we can keep it.*

CHAPTER 4

Divided States of America

Y OU MUST HAVE NOTICED – THERE'S A LOT OF DISAGREEMENT
and controversy out there. Think about how many times you have
disagreed with what people, both prominent and not so, have asserted
about America. An official, a politician, a cleric, an activist, an actor,
or your best friend may assert a position defining the nation, or assert
anything else for that matter, with which you're not in agreement.
Laws, policies, and governance are subject to many differing ideas
and priorities. Anyone can say what this nation stands for, but saying
it doesn't make it true.

We are a deeply divided nation. We always have been, and with
good fortune we always will be. Division and freedom of thought and
ideas are the natural way of things. In a totalitarian nation, unity of
thought is demanded. Dissention from state-prescribed thinking can
subject one to sanctions of more restricted living, imprisonment, or
death. Elections in Iran, Russia, Turkey, and other politically repressive regimes yielding popular votes for public officials at 90 percent
and above are the result and effect of thought containment, denial
of civil liberties, and extinction of humanity.

After an election in the United States, local, statewide, or national, with the winner getting 51 percent of the vote, from what until then had been a divided nation (or region), a typically ridiculous call for unity is made by the winning candidate. There must be something romantic about the idea of a battle royale of campaign-position wars ending in "the election now concluded, let's all come together." This is absurd. You don't change what you value just because the other side won. If your candidate/position lost the election, the only thing you think is "we have to win the next election."

There should always be honest reflection of what an election tells you. You should think harder about what happened and why the election went against the way you wanted. You should consider if there's a flaw in your understanding and positions. There is, however, after an election no requirement, nor is it necessarily wise, to "come together." But it is essential in a healthy, functioning republic and society to be civilized! Sinking to ad hominem attacks, specious haranguing, and straw-man fallacies only poisons any decent attempt at effective governance respecting the rights and liberty of its citizens.

African-American Voter Uniformity

In similar ways that the uniform 90-percent plus-vote in totalitarian regimes is problematic, the African-American plus 90-percent uniform vote for the Democratic Party's candidate is also problematic. For the U.S. presidency in 2000, the African-American vote was 90 percent for the Democrat candidate. In the 2004 presidential election the African-American vote was 88 percent for the Democrat candidate. In 2008 it was 95 percent. In 2012 it was 93 percent. And, in 2016 it was 89 percent. The Democratic Party deserves no congratulations for campaign excellence toward garnering African-American votes. Rather, it's shameful that (1) the Democratic Party has taken for granted the African-American vote, and (2), that as a group and to their detriment, African-Americans have allowed the Democratic Party to get away with identity/racial politics.

All other groups, such as other ethnicities, gender differences, age groups, and socioeconomic levels, are politically split much less disproportionally and closer to the fifty/fifty direction. This shows the more natural way division of thought is a normal occurring variance within and outside a group. Deliberately generated subsets of activism, special interests, classes of people, and identity politics is a more complicated matrix profile of division depending on the subset.

The only thing that should cause a significant disproportional vote is an almost unified rejection by voters of a candidate who is wildly absurd. It should not occur on racial lines – or with any other general groups.

A Little History

The egregious sin of slavery the Europeans brought to the new world in the Western Hemisphere has cursed our nation to this day. Even though all societies throughout history practiced slavery, including indigenous people of North America; even though the United States fought a civil war resulting in about 700,000 casualties, ultimately to end slavery; even though the Thirteenth Amendment to the U.S. *Constitution* abolished slavery, the legacy of slavery still touches us as foully today as any atrocity on a mass scale would.

After the Civil War, African-Americans who lived in the South were prevented from voting by Democrat white segregationists who governed, and were in complete control of, the Southern states. Those African-Americans who did vote, mostly voted Republican up through the first quarter of the twentieth century. The election of Franklin Delano Roosevelt to the presidency in1932 saw a change – more African-Americans now favored the Democrats. In the presidential elections of 1936, 1940, and 1944 the percentages for voting Democratic were as high as 71 percent. Even so, about half of African-Americans still identified as Republicans.

Before the 1948 election, President Harry Truman issued executive orders to desegregate the armed services and eliminate racial bias in federal employment. That election found that (1) for the first time the majority of African-Americans registered as Democrat, and (2) 77 percent of voting African-Americans voted for Truman.

In the subsequent presidential elections of 1952, 1956, and 1960 African-American vote percentages for Republicans ranged from 32 to 39 percent. But before the 1964 presidential election, Democratic president Lyndon B. Johnson pushed through the landmark Civil Rights Act of 1964. This act outlawed segregation in public places. The Republican candidate Senator Barry Goldwater was against the act. The Democrat got 94 percent of the African-American vote … a record.

President Lyndon Johnson later went on to sign the Voting Rights Act of 1965. Since 1964, no Republican presidential candidate has gotten more than 15 percent of the African-American vote.

Back to Now

It's undeniable and unavoidable that African-Americans have a historical standing that is profoundly different than any other group in this nation. The atrocity of three hundred years of slavery and subsequent institutional victimization and humiliation cannot be erased. It is precisely because of this ugly burden, we, as a society, must not cheapen the meaning of racism by reducing all human industry through the filter of racial and identity determinants. Ironically, if African-Americans continue to be a monolithic block they will continue to be politically exploited against their own best interests, as a group and as individuals. Freedom of thought and political philosophy needs to be restored to and regained by African-Americans.

Dark Divides

There are divides, and there are divides. There are the divides that occur naturally with variation of ideas, of creativity, and of intellectual depth – *vive la différence! – vive la divide!* Then there are "dark divides" that are the result of narrow, unwholesome, well-funded activist, organizations like *Media Matters*, the *Southern Poverty Law Center, MoveOn.org, Antifa,* and others that corrupt fairness and sensibility, while promoting cruelty and hatred against good people. Such organizations create a *toxic divide of destruction* by exploiting the mass of malcontents (see Chapter 3) and the dupes who join their ranks. This creates a malignancy of irrationality and absurdity throughout the world of *pop/political culture:* Man-made climate catastrophe will cause the planet to die in twelve years. Every woman in college is getting raped by white guys. African-Americans are going to be put back in chains. A woman has a right to do what she wants with her own body … and the body that just came out of her. Fire arms will be taken away from those who follow the law while those who break the law will continue possessing and using guns to victimize innocent people. "Correct" pronoun usage when referring to an individual will be mandatory, subject to penalty for violation. The means of production and distribution should be in control of government – socialism. And, unfortunately, the list goes on. Notice I said, malignancy in "the world of *pop/political culture*" – because this ideological malignant nonsense doesn't exist in the real world. However, this malignancy in *pop/political culture* is formidable and does affect the real world with its infusion of a *toxic divide of destruction* which seeks to destroy education, prosperity, freedom, medical care, creativity, infrastructure, compassion, the soul, the joy of living, institutions of growth, development, and support, and so many other good things in life.

The investigation of Trump and his campaign for president by a special prosecutor has also caused a *toxic divide of destruction*. As I write this, the special prosecutor's report has just been completed and turned over to the Department of Justice. The report recommended *no indictments* for collusion with Russia or obstruction of justice. But the corrupt, politically-driven reason for the investigation has already done severe harm. Ironically, our own politicians and media accomplished what the Russian government set out to do – disrupt and distract governance in America and reveal the stupidity, mental weakness, and vulnerability of the "dark divide" in America. The findings of the investigation were irrelevant to the purpose of disruption and distraction. Once the investigation was ordered there was no going back. No matter the findings, activist organizations, together with the mob of dupes, facilitated by anti-Trump media, already staked their intractable position on destruction. Despite the special prosecutor's report citing *no evidence* of collusion with the Russian government or obstruction of justice by the Trump campaign that would support indictments, the Trump opposition will not rethink its opinion, position, and actions. Instead, the Trump opposition has "tripled down" on their claims of Trump corruption, evilness, and illegitimacy. The Russian government took advantage of these self-destructive fools who hunger for the *toxic divide of destruction* ... yes indeed, *it's a republic, if you can keep it.*

CHAPTER 5

The First Amendment, Journalism, and Orwell

Congress shall make no law respecting an establishment of religion, or prohibiting the free exercise thereof; or abridging the freedom of speech, or of the press; or the right of the people peaceably to assemble, and to petition the Government for a redress of grievances.

THAT'S THE FIRST AMENDMENT. IT'S PACKED WITH A LOT OF stuff that establishes the essence of America. No other sovereign nation on the planet has so complete expression of freedoms as part of its governing principles. Only in America! Put another way – exceptionalism.

Hate Speech, Hate, and Libel

Hate speech is speech or any form of expression that attacks, threatens or insults a person or group on the basis of national origin, ethnicity, color, religion, gender, gender identity, sexual orientation, disability, or possibly things I can't think of now or haven't been thought of yet. Hate speech is not legal in Canada. Hate speech is legal in America.

Let's consider hate. Is hate good or bad? It should be obvious the question can't be answered without more information and context. The word "hate" is so charged it tends to emotionally strike "decent, nice people" as being bad. But a little maturity and sensibility would lead one to see hate is good or bad depending on what the word is referring to. If you hate poverty you've got it right. If you hate freedom without anarchy, you have a problem – a problem you're free to have in a free society.

What you can't do, even in America, is incite by way of any expression or communication physical violence against any person or groups of persons. Such would be a criminal act subject to imprisonment. Libel, a published false statement causing identifiable harm to a person or group with legal status, and slander, a spoken false statement causing identifiable harm to a person or group with legal status, are subject to civil action; if the offender is found responsible by a court of law, the offender could be ordered to pay a fine.

There is an imprecise exception that sort of looks past libel and slander against public figures. The rationale is public figures usually choose to be in the public eye. They, therefore, knowingly subject themselves to "the slings and arrows of outrageous" speech. Public figures in a sense tacitly assume the risk. But there have been cases in which public figures have successfully sued for damages resulting from libel and slander. These are defamation civil suits. Defamation is the same as libel and slander with one difference: it being, a defamatory statement can be made in any medium.

* * *

You're apt to love the First Amendment if it goes your way in any given situation, or hate it (there's that word "hate" again) if it works against you. But that's actually the point. The First Amendment is blind, like Lady Justice, to vile and disgusting things that are said as well as to uplifting and positive things that are said. The First Amendment is not devised for the benefit of an individual or faction or race of people. It's devised for the good of a republic – our Republic – in which each citizen has unalienable rights.

Despite the best understanding of the First Amendment, this nation, to this day, has not been able to avoid controversy about it. The Alien Sedition Acts, which John Adams, second President of the United States, signed into law, is widely considered the worst decision of his presidency. It may have been the reason he lost reelection to a second term. The Alien Sedition Acts, among many things, essentially prohibited public opposition to the federal government. Fines and imprisonment could be used against those who "write, print, utter, or publish … any false, scandalous, malicious writing" against the government.

So, pretty much right off the bat, when the nation was a "baby," the head of government President John Adams, who heroically risked his life, his fortune, and his sacred honor to help establish this unique country, dedicated to unalienable rights, insured by the stipulation of freedom of speech, canonized in not the Third, not the Second, but in the First Amendment to the *Constitution*, for which Adams swore an oath to … *preserve, protect and defend* … turned on his principles to gut freedom of speech out of the First Amendment.

You can see how fragile it is to preserve a right. Even people who would otherwise understand the profound consequences of essential principles, as Adams surely did, can be led away from them, as was Adams, when confronted with conflicting interests and challenges.

Let's Go to the Movies

In Frank Capra's 1939 movie *Mr. Smith Goes to Washington*, Jefferson Smith, played by Jimmy Stewart, is an idealistic patriot who is implausibly appointed to the U.S. Senate. Smith is not only idealistic, he's naïve. He humbly accepts the appointment to do his best to faithfully uphold the *Constitution* and represent his constituents. Alas, he is unaware and slow to learn his appointment is part of a political corruption that has been long in the making.

In his home state, Smith is the head of the Boy Rangers (sort of like Boy Scouts of America). Because of his values and interests, Smith innocently and earnestly works on a Senate bill he wants to propose for a federal government loan to buy land for a national boys' camp. *Side note:* This certainly isn't politically correct for today's societal climate. It should be a camp for … well all genders, ages, sexual self-identification, and whatever. Also, Smith's bill isn't even something the federal government should be getting into. But what the hey! It's Jimmy Stewart, ya gotta love it!

Smith's bill presents a problem for the big corrupt political machine. So the machine "turns the tables" on Smith by putting out misinformation and accusing Smith of his own brand of corruption and graft. *Another side note:* Boy, when you see what's going on today you realize when it comes to "snake in the grass" politics some things never change.

Throughout the movie, the press and media give Smith a hard time. He is stunned and emotionally defeated until he's rallied by his aide and Boy Ranger supporters to fight back. Facing a vote to expel him from the Senate, Smith launches a filibuster on the Senate floor to stall the vote. The Boy Rangers in his state mount an information campaign to prove Smith's innocence. But the big machine ruthlessly, violently, and criminally attacks the boys, shuts down their efforts, and ignites a media blitz of damning fake news against Smith. With the big machine pulling the strings, the press/media ultimately move to destroy Kavanaugh … I mean Smith.

In *Mr. Smith Goes to Washington*, controlling the message through the media is the corrupt political machine's weapon against Smith. The story shows the evils of political corruption – that corruption from special interests will surely occur at any cost, and that freedom of speech and a platform for it are the only way to call out corruption. It is why we must have a *free* and *honest* press.

As for Smith, Capra gave him and the people who root for the good guy a Hollywood ending (see Chapter 14). The only thing is, Smith's political mentor and hero who first betrayed Smith grows a conscience and dramatically breaks down, confessing his sins. That's never happened in politics … and it never will.

Let's Go to School

To reiterate: Freedom of speech and a platform for it are the only way to call out corruption. During the last ten years or so, colleges and universities have increasingly restricted their invitations to speakers. The restrictions are universally against speakers who are non-leftist, or leftists who are not pure and leftist enough. These restrictions are the result of leftist activist groups' ridiculous claims that speakers who are non-leftist or leftist-impure are messaging in hate speech. Though such claims are absurd, they are effective because school administrators cave to leftist activist-groups. There have been several Gestapo-like/fascists mob riots on campuses across the country, giving cover to administrators' claims of "campus violence" if non-leftist or non-pure leftists speakers speak. These spineless administrators, who may or may not be sympathetic to the leftist cause, allow themselves to be intimidated by the criminal actions of "the mob." Hiding behind the very real problem of unaddressed campus violence, these same administrators forego protective enforcement measures to make campuses safe for everyone, including non-leftist and non-pure leftist speakers.

Does this feel a bit like George Orwell's *1984?* Here's a quote from the novel, "If you want a picture of the future, imagine a boot stamping on a human face … forever." If campus administrators think it's dangerous to have speakers with a wide range of views and ideas presenting at campus forums, they might consider it's even more dangerous to restrict free speech and expression.

Hate speech is the go-to fallacious claim used by the left to shut down non-leftist, differing ideas. It piggy backs on the cause of political correctness (PC). Hate, particularly hate speech, is not PC. Orwell warns us as he describes no less than the death of humanity in *1984* – "Big Brother is watching you." That's another way of saying what PC is and does.

The idea of PC, as is the idea of Big Brother enacted, is the downfall of free speech, of our unalienable rights, of our Republic. Research conducted by *More in Common*, published in 2018, shows people across all demographics by wide margins strongly dislike "PC culture." A 2017 poll conducted by the CATO Institute found 71 percent of Americans said PC (in essence, Big Brother) has silenced important discussion our society needs to have.

Let's Go Out into the World

We have a free press. Thank goodness this was "baked" into the *Constitution* via the First Amendment. The free press is the only watchdog looking at government. Being "free," aside from the prohibition of inciting physical violence, destroying property, or committing libel and/or slander, means the free press can say, write, and otherwise express what it wants. The free press can and should do its job to alert us by focusing on what is relevant and needs attention; or it can fail us by promoting foolishness and "reshuffling the deck," making reality distorted and unrecognizable.

A free press is essential to our existence, but like nuclear power it can be a force of destruction. The press has never been more widespread and democratic than now. If you blog on the Internet, if you tweet on Twitter, if you post on Facebook, if you post videos on YouTube you are a part of the press. This book makes me part of the press. And if we are part of the press, as the cliché goes, we can be part of the problem or part of the solution. The press can be a tyranny for "group think" or a purveyor of unfiltered, raw, relevant information for competent and wise analysis – *part of the problem or part of the solution.*

Giants

At this time, there is no bigger information platform in the world, and as such no bigger public forum, than Google. Google owns YouTube. Google can block, reroute, or modify all the information you get. At this time, they can legally do that. As a private company they should be able to do that. But there are interesting questions as to what this means to freedom of the press, access for all of us, freedom of information, and freedom of speech.

With its prominence as the most-used and relied-on information platform in the world, Google is faced with the question as to whether the Google platform is a *de facto* public utility, subject to community regulation, or if their editorial control of content makes them in effect a publisher with private rights to do what they want with content, your content, your freedom of speech. Facebook and Twitter are looking at the same question. The answer to this question has serious ramifications for everyone on the planet ... it's a big deal!

Shadow blocking, also known as shadow banning, is when a person or organization posts content on a social network platform to be sent to the public at large, subscribers or other intended recipients, and the platform purposely fails to send the post. Moreover, the platform purposely keeps the sender unaware their post was not sent. Facebook and Twitter have been accused of this. They claim they don't have this policy practice, or if it has occurred at all it was an honest mistake.

As their controls and restriction decisions play out in public, YouTube clearly has a policy practice that's harder to deny. Their practices can be readily judged. YouTube responsibly has a setting that allows parents, guardians, and other adults in charge of minors, such as schools, to set the platform with a "restricted mode." This should prevent minors from viewing content that is not suitable for them because they're minors. But YouTube identifies content they don't like on the basis of YouTube's political biases and wrongly selects such content for the restricted mode. YouTube discriminates against such content not because it's inappropriate for minors, although that's what they implausibly claim. If anything, such reasonably legitimate content is highly educational and is exactly suitable for minors, particularly in this Republic.

These "book burning" issues show that ever-advancing technology creates challenging questions about maintaining our Constitutional rights, whether it's freedom of speech, the right to bear arms, or protection from government surveillances. In our Republic, the people, through their representatives under the provisions of the *Constitution* and *Bill of Rights*, work out these questions.

* * *

Indications are that Google/YouTube wants to indoctrinate the up-and-coming generation to ideology consistent with their corporate doctrines and world missions. Google's motto as of October, 2015, is "Do the right thing." Nothing wrong with that. But who decides what's right? Maybe, just maybe, there are different opinions on that matter. And, maybe having a healthy public discussion about Google and YouTube, with access to relevant information and freedom of speech to go with it, is the best possible way to advance our trajectory toward not only doing the right thing, but doing good.

In Orwell's allegorical novel, *Animal Farm*, published in 1945, the new societal doctrine devised by the animals on a farm is painted on the outside wall of the barn for all the citizen animals to see and live by. A pig, with a mind to rule this society for his own benefit, craftily maneuvers his takeover through thuggish, murderous violence, and propaganda messaging. He controls the message, which includes changes to the doctrine to suit himself and his fellow loyal pigs. In essence, what starts as a democratic revolt by the farm animals sets the table to enact new socialist/communist governance. But governance corruptly devolves into a singular authoritarian power which subverts the law – the doctrine. This subversion is prompted by state-owned press (rewritten/repainted doctrine on the side of the barn) and is brutally enforced by the pigs.

Let's Be Fair

If you control the message, you control … well, just about everything. Journalism is a messenger of messages. In some ways, journalism is *the* messenger of messages. In a fast paced, attention-deficit, product-branded culture/society, message consumption is much like mass-manufactured, processed food. It's not good for you and by extension not good for society and our Republic.

In a free society, although it may be expected by the public, journalism has no obligation or responsibility to do any specific thing. If journalism, or a journalist, wants to have a conscience and be critical/truthful, that's fine, but it's not a requirement, unless the brand is *credibility*. If you have a free-market republic, the free-market will decide the value of any journalistic product. To that purpose, journalism as a profession can adopt standards, but in any case it's the market that determines value. Unless the state takes over and violates the *Constitution*, you get the kind of journalism the market wants.

In 1949 the U.S. Federal Communications Commission (FCC) introduced the *Fairness Doctrine*, which was a policy requiring broadcast licensees to present controversial issues of public interest. The issues needed to be presented honestly, equitably, and balanced, as determined by the FCC. The *Fairness Doctrine* was ultimately eliminated as a policy in 1987. On its face, it may have seemed a perfectly reasonable regulatory measure. But its flaw was its being unworkable in a free society. The free market and market momentum weighed against the *Fairness Doctrine* as impractical, unusable, and not valuable. Having a bureaucratic institution decide what's fair cannot survive, because sooner or later the gravity of freedom will evoke the First Amendment, which has nothing to say about fairness. The chapter of history involving the *Fairness Doctrine* almost imperceptively exposes an implication of the First Amendment as it's not explicitly stated in the text of the amendment. That is – you are free to say what you want, and ... *here comes the implication* ... you are not compelled to say what you don't want to say – as the *Fairness Doctrine* required.

The First Amendment is a remarkable thing. It puts destiny simultaneously on our collective shoulders and individually on your shoulders as both a producer and consumer. Because of, and/or in spite of the First Amendment, we can go from liberty to Orwell in the blink of an eye and turn of the head. However it goes, journalism will have played an inseparable role. Yep, it's *"a republic, if you can keep it."*

CHAPTER 6

Fashion Over Reason

FASHION IS WHAT TELLS THE WORLD WHO AND WHAT a person is. If you wear T-shirts and jeans, you're telling the world something about you. If you say you're a registered Democrat or Republican or Independent, you're telling the world something about you. If you say you believe in free market principles, you're telling the world something about you. If you say you're a fan of the Dallas Cowboys football team, you're telling the world something about you. If you drive a BMW, you're telling the world something about you.

On a superficial level, the choices a person makes as to what they wear, drive, affiliate with, and believe from a fashion perspective may seem inconsequential. But this fashion variable has a deep consequence, as it profoundly relates to how you identify and define yourself. Fashion may seem like nothing more than a hair style, athletic shoes, a sports car, or window treatment. Fashion certainly includes these things that are more than just surface appeal. But at its core, fashion is who a person is both to their self and what they're saying to the world. And there is another psychological component to *fashion identification/adherence:* A person's need to be a part of a group or ethos brings about their willingness to give up their individual thoughts and beliefs – *fashion over reason.*

Consider someone who says they are Australian as the first way to describe them self. It's fashion that drives this identifier. Someone says they're a teacher as their first self-description. That's fashion speaking. It may be hard to see this as fashion because the person *is* Australian or *is* a teacher. You can think fashion can't change that, so fashion has nothing to do with it. The idea of fashion seems a little frivolous, like fingernail polish. That's why I'm pointing out what isn't readily seen or understood. Because fashion is everything we really care about. And fashion does change or inform how we think and where we stand in any particular moment.

Take the word "brand." Fashion is a function of brand. It can be a traditional, well-known brand or a new brand in the making. The brand can be authentic or fake. But the brand is essential to the fashion; and the need for a fashion is what we crave to satisfy. This satisfaction in politics is by way of tribal affiliation with a brand.

Let's try this out on some politics. Barack Obama has always been well-liked and popular. People like liking him. And, it's *fashionable* to like him. The charismatic pull Obama has on people happens for a matrix of reasons. But whatever the reasons, which are the campaign pitches the electorate buys into, the *effect* is what causes the alignment of full-throated, fully-committed political tribal affiliation with the Obama brand. What's the *effect?* The *effect* is that composite reasons become condensed, reduced, and simplified to a fashion, the fashion, on which you stake your very self-identified existence. It's a very big deal!

In November of 2008 Barack Obama said, "I believe marriage is between a man and a woman. I am not in favor of gay marriage."

On the May 6, 2012 broadcast of *Meet the Press* Vice President Joe Biden got in front of then President Obama and said in effect same-sex marriages should be recognized legally. Politically, this forced Obama's hand to get on board with an "evolved" position on the matter in support of same-sex marriage. No matter what Obama really thought to himself about same-sex marriage, he had to keep his fashion recognition popular and forward; he had to make the shift. This was pure and not so simple, a fashion calculation. The pro-same-sex marriage people and President Obama needed each other to strengthen and advance their respective and mutual "brand" interests. They essentially became each other's fashion accessory. What anyone in the vast electorate thought or believed about this matter and how it played out with Obama was ultimately a fashion decision by the politicians, the media, and the electorate.

Decisions, your decisions, are made based on how it looks and with which "fashion tribe" you want to affiliate.

* * *

To run anything effectively, a business, a family, a high school prom, a republic, you need to make policy decisions. It's remarkable how every position to take or decision to make is controversial. If a community wants to put up a public park in the middle of town someone is going to be against it. So, in a republic with democratic features such as elections, town hall meetings, initiatives, and so on, the process of working out decisions is enacted. However, and this is important, all decisions to be considered and made are subject to being hijacked by fashion adherence instead of adherence to the critical factors involved in policy details. Fashion is all-consuming. It supersedes actual policy details to the point that policy is lost or at least rendered secondary. *Fashion takes the place of substance.* It's similar to what political strategist Lee Atwater said, "perception is reality." Or as Marshall McLuhan put it, "the medium is the message." So, in this way we might say, "fashion is the issue."

Fashion is what drives discussion, debate, arguments, and invectives on all the big-scale current issues – the economy, taxes, guns, abortion, immigration, race, gender, gender identification, foreign policy, radical Islamic terrorism, climate change, and health care. If you simply look at the divide based on right wing vs. left wing positions on any of these issues, the opposition begins, and often ends, with their attacking your fashion tribe. If the right favors a park in the middle of town, the left will call it "racism." If the left favors a park in the middle of town, the right will call it "socialism." Whatever are the pros and cons of a park are lost to the *non sequitur*, irrelevant, and erroneous sleight-of-hand afforded by the fashion smoke screen. Against your political opposition, your political enemy, you can "reverse fashion" them. You can brand them something undesirable, such as racist, socialist, or whatever. This is one of the features of fashion.

In the fierce take-no-prisoners public discourse, you can be a "fashion cop" (as in "fashion police") or a "fashion warrior" against your opposition. You can "fashion shame" them. These tactics are low and disreputable and often backfire; but the take-away for our discussion and understanding is the wholesale reduction of who we are, whether fairly or wrongly applied, comes down to *fashion*.

The Lens

John F. Kennedy is one of the presidents who reached icon status in the minds of Americans who think about presidents. He was charismatic, mysterious, and accessible in a Rorschachian kind of way. That is, then and now we can make him be what we want him to be. Most people forgive Kennedy's imperfections no matter what they know or don't know of such, and see him in a positive way, as a good man and very good president. We like to imagine the world would have been better if he hadn't been assassinated.

This generalized collective impression of Kennedy is the fulfillment of the fashion narrative that continues strongly long after his death. The fashion narrative today is Kennedy was a good person and as a Democrat a champion of liberal principles. Today, there may be many who even think he is a great example for progressivism. However, Kennedy's political philosophy aligned with conservatism; his fiscal policies were conservative by today's standards, as well as in his time. During his administration, the military budget increased while other federal expenditures were restrained. He pushed for tax cuts, arguing it would increase government revenue. The cuts were enacted months after Kennedy's assassination. His predictions were realized as the tax cuts contributed to, as Marilyn Geewax wrote for NPR, "… one of the most robust economic expansions in history." Kennedy believed in free trade; he lowered tariffs; he was for a free market; he was an ardent opponent of communism. In other words, Kennedy's real political ethos was almost opposite of liberalism. This shows another way fashion functions. What we see is dependent on the "fashion lens" we view it through. If we have a stake in valuing liberal over conservative we then have a liberal fashion lens with which to see, and vice versa if we view things through a conservative fashion lens.

It's noteworthy how history is reconstructed – per Kennedy – to suit fashion. That's the overriding effect of fashion adherence. If you're part of a political tribe you want to claim positive, successful icons as of your own. But if an icon was successful with policies and principles different than those of your own and your tribe you have a bit of a cognitive dissonance problem. Well, not to worry. You really don't have a problem if you don't let facts get in the way and you just stick with your fashion. You can always – per Kennedy – accessorize to make your philosophy look like it fits with fashion and good policy. Additionally, you can just go feelings-based with your fashion. After all, feelings are always reliable.

* * *

When fashion-driven choices replace what should be relevance-driven choices, positions are espoused through fashion, not, all importantly, through issues, principles, and critical thinking. Emotions replace reason. An example is the often espoused cliché "America is a nation of immigrants." This simplistic "fashion bumper sticker" is supposed to pass as an immigration policy encompassing all the complexities associated with serious immigration challenges and problems. The policy statement is really a fashion statement. And, at this point the espouser isn't even aware of it!

Philosopher, essayist, and novelist, George Santayana wrote, *"Fashion is something barbarous, for it produces innovation without reason and imitation without benefit."*

In the words Shakespeare gave to Cicero in the play *Julius Caesar* *"... men may construe things after their fashion, clean from the purpose of the things themselves."*

PART II

THE TRUMP THING

T HE ELEPHANT IN THE ROOM IS DONALD TRUMP. ONLY WITH this elephant everybody's talking about it all the time. Whether we dislike him, despise him, or like him, love him, we can't get enough of him. There are few times in all history that a person, in their own time, so dominated the collective psyche.

Due to the Internet, the fully-loaded and utilized 24-hour news cycle, the stream of cable television punditry programming, radio, podcasts, and social media it's possible by some metrics that Trump is the most provocative and widely-known person in real time throughout the world – more than anybody so far in history. That's pretty remarkable.

A result of this unprecedented ubiquitous presence is so much thought, feeling, and talk about this person. Or, so much thought, feeling, and talk causes this unprecedented ubiquitous presence.

Either way, this energy feeds on itself; it's in perpetual motion and it's growing. With so much being thought, felt, and talked about Trump there is much more being processed "badly" than in a sensible, measured, and healthy manner. Part II of this book will contribute to the "good" processing of *the Trump thing*.

CHAPTER 7

Why Trump Won

TECTONIC SHIFTS OF CONTINENTAL MOVEMENT ON THE planet occur without any regard for the politics of people. These are bold physical occurrences that are completely independent of the wisdom or foolishness of human kind.

When I'm in the company of one person or a group of people, I always start off cautiously if Trump's name is spoken or the subject of Trump is brought up. It is for way too many people an instantaneous non-starter litmus test for what is to come of my (and your) relationship with these people. It has happened in my clinical work with patients, business associates, family members, friends, and acquaintances. This litmus test is simply dangerous and destructive because reason is abandoned and replaced with absolute adherence to anti-Trumpism. There is no place to move, breathe, or think. It is disheartening, because the "world of possibility," where hope lives, is utterly extinguished. The anti-Trumpers do not see their reactionary views and behavior as a shut-down of "possibility" because they are blinded by their self-righteousness. Their absolute certainty of their righteousness is fueled by Trump's rawness and what they consider his vulgarity, his political oppositions' labeling-campaign against him, and the mainstream oppositional press.

So when I find myself in a situation where the subject of Trump comes up, as a cause to slay the "devil," I either do not engage the subject and let it go or, if I'm willing to be adventurous, I offer up a question to see if I can prompt some thought over emotion. I ask, "Despite who and what Trump is, do you know why he was elected?" This usually pauses the discussion. Once we get past the theories about the Russians, the FBI, Trump-bought-the-election, the Electoral College, and so on, all of which interestingly enough are easy to get past, we land on the reason Trump got elected.

The reason Trump won was he saw the "tectonic shift" and campaigned on it. Trump said, "Make America Great Again." Hillary didn't say anything. She had an amorphous voice say, "I'm With Her." What Hillary and her surrogates did say was Trump was a racist, a bigot, a misogynist, and all the other despicable things a bad person would be. Then she went further, she called Trump supporters "deplorable." Nice touch.

Trump took a chance: He took a chance that the thoughtful voter would find Hillary's rhetoric on his nature, his character, and his despicableness insulting to their collective intelligence. He took a chance that we could criticizes him, disagree with him, identify his weaknesses and short comings, but that enough of us would not buy into the litany of claims the Hillary camp was spewing. The Hillary campaign, together with all the anti-Trumpers on all sides, *didn't* focus on what the electorate through the "refining filter" of the Electoral College cared about! Trump *did!* That's why he won.

* * *

With rabid anti-Trumpers, it's an easier discussion to simply point out, without even saying you're for Trump (whether you are or not), that Trump does a better job delivering on what most of the electorate – the people – care about, whereas his political opponents have abandoned what most people care about. Moreover, his opponents are stuck on the shock of his election and obsessed with undoing the past through investigations, the legal apparatus, the political mechanism of impeachment, and a media propaganda campaign to expose things (true or fake) that most of the electorate don't care about.

If the Trump opposition wants Trump out they should use the election process. That's what it's for. All they need to do is put up a candidate with a message most of the voters care about and convey the confidence the candidate can deliver. By all evidence, this is not the way they're going. It looks as though when the 2020 election comes around they're going to triple down on their last campaign rhetoric. So, if this happens, like the last election, Trump will have not done it to them, they will again have done it to themselves.

As I said, asking why Trump won is the best way I know to engage and maneuver in a discussion with an anti-Trumper. This question is designed to be both civil and thoughtful, allowing for mutual intellectual and moral integrity. With this approach to the discussion, I find even the most rabid anti-Trumpers will agree Hillary lost the election for lack of vision and Trump won because he understood the electorate and played the "cards" correctly.

Michael Moore, a Man with a Purpose

The foundational reason Trump won – that he understood the electorate – is well-illustrated in a presentation Michael Moore gave shortly before the 2016 November election. Moore cares about his politics enough not to lie to himself about what his side (anti-Trumpers) was missing. What his side was missing was: Trump was connecting to enough people to beat Hillary and win the election. I'm not a fan of Michael Moore, but I am a fan of good analytical thinking no matter where it comes from. Moore provided one of the most street-wise, eloquent, gritty analyses of the Trump candidacy. His opposition to Trump made his assessment all the more credible.

Moore's oration to a large audience on his analysis is worth reading. So here it is:

Donald Trump came to the Detroit Economic Club and stood there in front of a [sic] Ford motor executives and said, "If you close these factories, as you're planning to do in Detroit, and build them in Mexico, I'm going to put a 35-percent tariff on those cars when you send them back, and nobody's going to buy them." It was an amazing thing to see. No politician, Republican or Democrat, had ever said anything like that ... to these executives. And it was music to the ears of people in Michigan and Ohio and Pennsylvania and Wisconsin – the "brexit states." You live here in Ohio. You know what I'm talking about. Whether Trump means it or not is kind of irrelevant because he's saying the things to people who are hurting. And it's why every beaten-down, nameless, forgotten working stiff, who used to be part of what was called the middle class loves Trump. He is the human molotov cocktail that they've been waiting for. The human hand grenade that they can legally throw into the system that stole their lives from them. And on November 8th, election day, although they lost their jobs, although they've been foreclosed on by the bank, next came the divorce, and now the wife and kids are gone, the car has been repoed [sic], they haven't had a real vacation in years, they're stuck with a shitty Obama care bronze plan, when you can't even get a fucking Percocet. They essentially lost everything they had! Except one thing. The one thing that doesn't cost them a cent, and is guaranteed to them by the American *Constitution* – the right to vote! They might be penniless, they might be homeless, they might be fucked-over and fucked-up. It doesn't matter. Because it's equalized on that day. A millionaire has the same number of votes as the person without a job – one. And there's more of the former middle class than there are in the millionaire class. So on November 8th, the dispossessed will walk into the voting booth, be handed a ballot, close the curtain, and take that lever or felt pen or touch screen, and put a big fucking "X" in the box by the name of the man who has threatened to up-end and over-turn the very system that has ruined their lives – Donald J. Trump! They see that the elites, who ruined their lives, hate Trump. Corporate America hates Trump. Wall Street hates Trump. The career politicians hate Trump. The media hates Trump. After they loved him, and created him, and now hate him. Thank you, media. The enemy of my enemy is who I'm voting for on November 8th. Yes, on November 8th you, Joe Blow, Steve Blow, Bob Blow, Billy Blow, Billy Bob Blow, all the Blows get to go and blow up the whole God damn system because it's your right. Trump's election is going to be the biggest "fuck you" ever recorded in human history. And it will feel g-o-o-d.

Let's make clear what Moore is doing here with an analysis of his analysis. Let's also understand the context of psychology and the attempt by Moore to psychologically process what is for him, as it is for those of his ilk and for those whom he would like to persuade to join his ilk, an unacceptable reality – Trump's legitimate election to the presidency. Here we go ...

It is first necessary to say where Moore is coming from in terms of his world view and his politics. To describe this, it immediately occurred to me I was going to get it wrong if I said the obvious – he is a radical left-wing socialist activist. Moore is something much more than that. He is a *malcontent*. Moore has contempt for those who hold power over the system, whether it's the capitalist corporate bosses or the state-controlled bureaucracy. The basis of his malcontentedness is the idea the system always screws the "little guy." I actually like Moore better and find some agreement with him if I use this more complicated and complete description than if I simply dismiss him as a left-wing extremist. *Side note to all of us:* It's better and more accurate not to dismiss anyone with an un-nuanced, one-dimensional epithet – like referring to someone as a racist, bigot, misogynist, homophobe, left-winger, right-winger, so on and so on. Even if those descriptions are accurate for that person, a rule of thumb is such descriptors should only be used by a person to describe them self. It isn't necessary for you to weigh in on a person with unflattering ad hominem labels – always and still a major problem in public discourse.

Anyway, Moore is caught between a rock and a hard place. He has no place to go. So, he uses his public platform and his brand to cathartically resolve what cannot be resolved in his head: Trump's appeal is undeniable to people like Moore or those with whom he identifies – the "working stiff." This identification causes cognitive dissonance in Moore. And cognitive dissonance is an ugly thing in an activist because it's bad enough when someone disagrees with an activist, but when an activist has thoughts that disagree their own activism they project anger and double down! Moore genuinely understands the appeal Trump has on the "working stiff," whom Moore loves. Moreover, he is furious the political campaign against Trump was such a failure because Trump showed he hears these people and Hillary was "deaf" to them. Hillary and her camp took Trump for granted and, worse, took the "little-guy/working-stiff" for granted.

In all of this, however, Moore makes an unjustified assumption: the dispossessed "working stiff" is motivated to "blow-up" the system as revenge for being screwed-over. What Moore fails to acknowledge, as if it doesn't or couldn't possibly exist, is the "little guy" may actually like Trump, may see him as a guy they were always looking for and instead of his blowing up the system, Trump is going to remake the system to make it work the way it's supposed to. It's captured perfectly in Trump's brand – "Make America Great Again."

This would be a double cognitive dissonance for Moore because (1) Moore does not see Trump as a good guy, and (2) as some kind of socialist, Moore has contempt for capitalism and doesn't believe the system should work the way it's supposed to – as a capitalistic system. By the way, to his credit, Moore has done very well in this capitalistic/freedom-of-speech system.

Voter Appeal and Election Strategy

Ironically, Trump won the election for president for the same reason Obama was elected president and reelected for a second term. They both, in their own way, connected to enough people. Hillary tacitly, and embarrassingly, consented to run as "Obama's third term."

The problem for Hillary, however, was the electorate liked Obama, but not necessarily his policies. He ran on pure charisma.

Hillary started out with a huge stack of unearned "chips." There was no policy, no vision, and certainly no charisma. Hillary, counseled by her advisors, ran only on – it was *her* turn. The strategy was to avoid mess-ups, to remind everybody Hillary's a woman and Bill used to have charisma, and not to make bold assertions charting a course for the future. Then let the stack of chips run down, but not all the way; by the time of the election there would still be enough chips to win. This was part of the strategy against Bernie Sanders for delegate-votes for the party's nomination. That time it worked … barely. But for her contest against Trump, there weren't enough chips left. She busted-out!

If the electorate allows a party, an office holder, or one who seeks office to take its votes for granted, our Republic won't survive. After all, it's "*a republic, if you can keep it.*"

CHAPTER 8

An Interview with President Trump, Imagined

A Fake Interview, a Real Profile of Donald Trump

THE CLICHÉ ABOUT STEPPING INTO SOMEONE'S SHOES to better understand who they are, what motivates them, and their manner of conversational speech is a valid and useful device for "point of view" comprehension. It is an exercise an expert in forensics can conduct.

In my work with individuals, couples, and groups, particularly those with business and political conflicts, I often act out a vignette about some issues that are of interest. I play all the parts (all the people I'm working with – it's validating to those who have felt alienated and not understood). When I finish a vignette I ask everyone I portrayed if I got it right – did I project a fair and accurate essence of respective positions, thoughts, and feelings? This exercise is a powerful tool, creating mutual understanding for those who participate, particularly where there has been serious disagreement and conflict between and among the participants.

The following is the product of this kind of exercise. If you factor in a person's profile, motivations, psychology, cognitive/intellectual presentation, and personality style, a faithful interactional dialogue can be constructed.

This is a forensic profile exercise. I express my own voice not as a psychotherapist but as an opinion journalist, and I portray President Donald Trump based on an authentic public profile. This conversational interview <u>did not</u> happen... but it could have. "A" is for me (Asher), "T" is for Trump

* * *

A: Hi, Mr. President, thanks for taking the time to talk with me. I've been eager to ask some questions I don't think you've been asked.

T: Sure, let's do it.

A: OK, what do you think about this "Trump" phenomenon?

T: "Trump" phenomenon?

A: Yeah, "Trump" phenomenon. The current *pop/political climate* can't even be considered without acknowledging the "Trump" effect, the "Trump" factor ... the "Trump" phenomenon.

T: Well, there's never been anything like it. There're four parts to it. There's me, there's the people, there's the "swamp," and there's the "fake news."

A: Those last two things were labels you came up with, "swamp" and "fake news."

T: Yeah, I'm good at branding. The whole idea of branding is to deliver a message that gets to the point. The officials who are running Washington government have created a swamp. It's ineffective, inefficient, wasteful, and corrupt. The fake news is allowing it. They're not doing their job. Before I was a candidate for president, the media loved me. When I became a candidate, they loved me. I'm a ratings hit for them. I'm more a ratings hit now than before and their programming would be in the tank if it weren't for me. But when I won the nomination, they got scared, because the swamp they supported was going to be challenged by me. So, the fake news media, which is most of them – not all, but most of them – ginned-up their propaganda against me. It's actually against the people, since I was fairly elected.

A: Actually, there's a formidable challenge to the idea that you were fairly elected.

T: Yep, see what I mean? The swamp works hand-in-hand with the fake news as well as corrupt leaders in the FBI and the Justice Department. That's what I and the American people are up against. So, here's how the fake news would report what I just said to you about the FBI and Justice Department – *Trump is against the good men and women of the FBI and the Department of Justice. Trump is against the press and the First Amendment.* It's a lie and they know it. The fake press has no respect for the American people. I'm betting that the people aren't fooled by the fake press. I'm betting on the people.

A: You used the word "lie" to say what the "fake press" does. You're called a liar every day. *The most lying president in history.*

T: Yeah, it's amazing. Again, it's a part of the swamp/fake news thing. It's the pot calling the kettle black. The lies that come out of that muck is what it feeds on. It's self-feeding.

A: Well, they would say that's what you're doing.

T: At some point, no matter what is said by whomever, the people will see who is saying what is truthful and what matters most in their lives. You can take anything I say and if you're corrupt you can twist the meaning to make it be something very different than my real message. People see that for the first time someone, that's me, is calling the fake press out. And they, the press and media, don't like it. I'm not worried. The people can see who is credible and who shouldn't be trusted.

A: Even so, you are a negative trigger for about half the country.

T: Look, I get it, I'm not everybody's cup of tea. I got a big ego, I'm a bigger than life character, sue me. No wait, don't sue me; I have enough of that already. I actually don't think the number of people who dislike me is as high as they say. Many people, and I think the percentage is high, are "closet" Trump supporters. They can't be open with their approval and support because they will suffer bad consequences from lunatic Trump-haters around them. It's cruel and it's sad.

A: Mr. President, regarding your tax returns, why don't you just say you're never going to release them to the public because it's nobody's business? It's between you and the IRS. If the IRS has any issues they can take it up with you privately. Also, politically it's stupid to release them. It's just "red meat" for your political enemies. Given the complexities of your vast holdings, why subject yourself to the scrutiny of those who are against you and don't understand the tax code? The general public won't take the time to understand it either. Why don't you just say that?

T: What you're saying makes sense. Let's see what happens.

A: You know your opposition is going to keep bothering you about this.

T: They're going to bother me no matter what I say or do. But I think what you said is a good reason why nobody should release tax information. Presidential candidates started doing it … I think

Nixon or Carter. Anyway, the media and swampy politicians treat it like it's a requirement to release tax returns.

A: That's my point. You have a chance to reset how the electorate sees and understands how releasing tax information is not only not required, it's unreliable and confounding in what it tells, and wholly unnecessary.

T: Yep, let's see what happens.

A: So, with every political and policy success you have, opposition to Trump intensifies. You're attacked with harsher rhetoric and accusations. Is that a problem?

T: Well, first of all, they're not my successes, they're the country's successes. But I know what you mean. Democrats and liberals have been hijacked by various leftist fringe that are powerful and manipulative. They get me, and they're afraid my presidency will defeat their leftist political goals and their power. They're right. Because the American people can see right through them and I've shown that I know how to deal with them by calling them out the way that I do. Their message is a lie. They've managed to run things for decades. The party's over. And they're very angry.

A: Trade, guns, manufacturing jobs, abortion, the flag, tweets, climate, law enforcement, the wall, acting presidential, Chicago, immigration, opioid crisis, the national debt, radical islamoterrorism, racism, Russia, natural disasters, Google, and so on have all been politicized. It seems that it's one thing to have different opinions about issues and things, but it's another to see everything through a political prism.

T: That's how cynical we've gotten. Or, maybe it's always been that way, but it spreads wider and more toxically because of the 24-hour fake news cycle. I think my presidency is really important, not because of me, but because the country has been waiting so long to get back to the founding principles that make this nation exceptional and a hope for the world. I'm a disrupter of the bad things that hold this nation back. I don't lead from behind. Before my presidency is done, I believe we will go far to minimize cynicism.

A: You get a lot of criticism from your political opponents about how you conduct foreign policy.

T: If Obama did what I'm doing they'd be praising him. It's not my foreign policy they have a problem with, it's me. It's not so much what I do, it's that they are so invested in their extreme hatred for me that anything I do, even when it is obviously good, they trash it.

A: In a short time span, you've had a lot of turnover in your cabinet and White House senior staff. Could you talk about that?

T: It's simple; I believe in "good-hire/good-fire." I'm very grateful to those who served. Most all of them are great people, exceptional for what they do. But appointing someone involves more than getting a great, qualified person. It has to be a great fit. And you can't really know until they are on the job. I'm not afraid to make changes when it's necessary. You should expect more down the road. My cabinet and staff know that; they're good people; they're professionals. This aspect of leadership and management highlights something that people are frustrated about regarding government. It's been asked, "shouldn't we run government like a business?" And I think some things in government should definitely be run more like a business. If there's anyone who knows how to run businesses, it's me. I'm sure that was one of the reasons I was elected. I get results. In business you have to be accountable for productivity and profits. If you're not productive and profitable, you're out of business. For much too long, government programs continue to exist even though they're costly with no benefit or good results. Business has to face up to failures, government doesn't ... at least in the "swamp," they don't. Government, like business, needs to see its successes and its failures. We need to make and keep government accountable. The VA is a good example. It was disgraceful and criminal the way veterans were treated, or not treated, in the system. I signed the *VA Mission Act* which among many things allows veterans to get medical attention in existing private care programs so they don't die standing in line at VA facilities. On top of that I signed the new *VA Accountability and Whistleblowers Protection Act*. It lets us clean up incompetence and/or corrupt government personnel. Imagine how ridiculous this wasn't fixed a long time ago. The swamp didn't even address it until I got into office ... disgraceful.

A: That got you wound up.

T: You bet it does.

A: So, how does it look for the rest of your term.

T: Well, I've already said I'm running for reelection, so I'm looking at the long haul. Just keep your seat belt on. It's going to be a bumpy ride because the Dems have made their only strategy and their only message anti-Trump. And they have the fake news to carry their water. I don't know, maybe they'll learn I'm a nice guy, I can work with them if they wouldn't be so small-minded and stupid. I can make things better for them ... for everybody. But probably not; they just won't get it. Too bad. It's a shame.

A: OK, Mr. President, that wraps it up. I really appreciate the time you gave to talk with me. Thank you.

T: I'm happy to have met with you. You're respectful, not snarky like I get from Trump-hating journalists. Those were good questions. You're a very smart guy.

* * *

If Donald Trump reads this, I would appreciate hearing from him to let me know if I got it right. He can validate, modify, or dispute my projections. I aim to be accurate and faithful to his opinions, thoughts, and feelings. If I have failed in this, I apologize to Donald Trump and my readers … But I'm pretty sure I nailed it. Particularly, the part where he calls me smart.

(^‗‘)

CHAPTER 9

The Emperor's New Clothes
And the Emperor is not Trump

MESSAGING IS THE "IT" IN LEADERSHIP. THE SLOGANS PRESIDENTIAL candidates are known for tell so much, if not everything, about the candidate. Effective slogans distill the vast complexity of political philosophy, values, and personal temperament into a few words that convey, "here's all you need to know." That's what slogans are for.

Let's look at the greatest hits of Barack Obama, Hillary Clinton, and Donald Trump:

Barack Obama said, "Hope and Change." Well "hope" is a nice word. "Change" is all right if that's what you want. But what if that's not what you want. Five days before the 2008 election candidate Obama said, "We are five days away from fundamentally transforming the United States of America!" When we have elections we are choosing an executive to run things, using the *Constitution* as a foundation already set. We just want the executive to run things well, not fundamentally change the system that elected him or her.

Earlier, candidate Obama said, "… like a lot of small towns in the Midwest, the jobs have been gone now for twenty-five years and nothing's replaced them … each successive administration has said that somehow these communities are going to regenerate, and they have not. Well it's not surprising then that they get bitter and *they clung* [sic] *to guns or religion* or antipathy toward people who aren't like them or anti-immigrant sentiment or anti-trade sentiment … a way to explain their frustrations."

The line that surfaced, getting much public attention as an insulting *faux pas* was, "they clung [sic] to guns or religion." It was that line that drew me to research the recording. I had not heard the entire commentary before. In its entirety, Obama's opinions and comments are much worse than I knew. They show a real contempt, disrespect, and prejudice against people in general. As for the "guns or religion" line, people who don't like guns or religion may be pleased with a leader who also doesn't like them. Or thinks guns and religion are overrated, or … I don't know, what is the message?

President Obama, said, "… if you've got a business … you didn't build that. Somebody else made that happen." He essentially diminished, or discounted altogether, all entrepreneurs' industry, hard work, vision, personal risk, and value brought to the community at large. That message was clear and came with a "slap in the face."

Hillary Clinton said, "I'm With Her." Sounds like you've shown up at a back stage after-party that Hillary has a pass for. The guy at the door in charge of who gets in looks at Hillary's pass and then looks at you. You say, "I'm with her."

Hillary said, "You can put half of Trump supporters into what I call the basket of deplorables … the racist, sexist, homophobic, xenophobic, Islamophobic … you name it." The message to all of the Trump supporters is there is no limit to how bad you are! *Side note:* And, what should we think about the other half?

Donald Trump said, "Make America Great Again." "Make" is not "Hope." "Hope" is passive, wishful, and uncertain. "Make" is an action word. "America," that's the whole target, that's every American citizen. "Great" is the highest, most positive state of being. "Again" reminds us that we are great, but corruption and foolishness can and were bringing us down … *"A republic, if you can keep it."*

Trump said, "Drain the swamp." He rightly called the state of affairs practiced by dishonest, incompetent public officials in governance and politics a "swamp." There's no misunderstanding the meaning of swamp as derogatory: a quagmire and morass of political, bureaucratic entrenchment serving only special interests. "Drain" is also an action word. The message is to rid governance of incompetence and corruption … *"A republic, if you can keep it."*

Trump said, "Fake news." The message is junk in, junk out. The mainstream media is more than the network of newspapers, television, radio, podcasts, internet, and social media platforms. As a whole, mainstream media is determinately left-leaning. And, as such, reported events have a different meaning, sometimes very different, that is, fake, than would be if left-wing politics and sentiments were absent. Commentary is fine, but commentary passing for news is disingenuous, undermining critical analysis … *"A republic, if you can keep it."*

The media, which is overwhelmingly and disproportionately anti-Trump, criticizes him for all manner of things, all the while acting as if the "sanctity" of journalism is above criticism. The full context for Trump slamming this media faction is based on what he not only considers but outright calls fraudulent reporting – *fake news.* This media faction believes it can criticize Trump, impugn his motives without any benefit of doubt, asserting the worst about him; and according to this media faction, Trump is not allowed to fire back … he fires back.

Notwithstanding, Trump out-messaged his political opponents. And he out-messaged the anti-Trump media. His message showed a proactive and positive vision. He branded the anti-Trump media by hanging the word "fake" on it. And, they can't shake it off. The anti-Trump media are enraged by Trump's one-upmanship, making them more hysterically determined to take him down – with propaganda they call news. Yet, every time they claim to report news, Trump says, "fake."

* * *

Hans Christian Andersen's story, *The Emperor's New Clothes*, is an allegory about, among many things, how people can be led by fakery. People will buy into things that aren't true or real because of self-serving vanity and fashion (as discussed in Chapter 5), as well as insecurity.

The Emperor's New Clothes is about a ruler who's obsessed with being ridiculously well-dressed. He changes his attire several times a day. He spares no cost to do this, at the expense of every other thing important and essential for running the state of affairs in his kingdom.

Two swindlers see an opportunity to make a killing financially, and maybe to make a point. They pose as weaver/tailors and come to the ruler with an offer he can't refuse. They will make the best outfit out of the best material that had ever been made in all history. Moreover, the swindlers say the outfit will be invisible to anyone who is unfit in their job and off-the-chart stupid. The swindlers explain the work will be demanding and that the thread is unique and so exquisite, the cost will be very much more than ever spent for a suit of clothes.

That should have been a giveaway. Instead, the ruler is even more committed to the engagement and the cost. Not only in his twisted vanity mind will he look more *fantastic* than anyone ever has, he will know who around him is incompetent and a fool. (Hey king, you want to know who's a fool? Look in the mirror. I'm sure you have one... sorry, I got carried away.)

The swindlers get right to work. They set up two looms, but they don't really weave any fabric. They make pantomime motions pretending to weave fabric. Anyone watching them work see no fabric, but out of fear of being humiliated and fired from their job they don't say anything except how great the fabric looks.

After much anticipation, the swindlers announce completion of the suit of clothes. The ruler and his ministers proclaim this to be such an important event that a public procession is declared so the ruler can show off his new outfit.

For the public procession, the swindlers "dress" the ruler in the new "clothes." Again, they pantomime the motions of dressing the ruler. Everyone present, including the ruler, is pretty uncomfortable. But nobody admits to seeing nothing. The ruler is completely naked, yet everyone says how great the outfit looks. Wow!

So in all his naked glory, the ruler goes forth to the procession to show off his new "threads" to all his subjects. Everyone throughout the land hears the outfit will be invisible to fools. At first the crowd is mostly silent, with the only audible comments being how great the clothes look. That all changes when a kid in the crowd, about eleven years in age, yells out, "Hey, man, the dude is naked! He's not wearing a damn thing!" The kid, without reservation or concern about being thought of as stupid, yells out reality and the truth. Moreover, the kid shows what is really stupid is believing in and going along with nonsense. With that, the crowd's cognitive dissonance goes from individually-internal to collectively-outward. Things get worse, or better, depending on your perspective.

* * *

The Emperor's New Clothes parallels the current drift to corruption, or the "swamp," as Trump calls it. In the story, the ruler is fixated on something irrelevant and self-serving. In the real world, the swamp and the media are "wearing" the emperor's new clothes. At least half of our public officials are almost singularly focused on the straw-man of anti-bigotry/identity-political rhetoric. All issues are subjected to the political-correctness filter. Like the fear people had in the story of being a fool if the clothes are invisible to the observer, you can't say, let alone think, anything deemed politically incorrect. Remember, *the kid* yells reality and truth. Donald Trump is *that kid*. The analogy of the kid to Trump is all the more fitting because of Trump's kidlike way of talking, at times crude, simple, unfiltered. Though Trump can be inarticulate too, his meaning is clear, truthful, and sophisticated to sensible ears.

Conversely, to the ears of anti-Trumpers his way of talking is "red meat." They can take what Trump says and how he says it and mold it to suit their intractable, horrific view of him. To be sure, Trump too often says things that would have been better unsaid not just for political reasons, but because they're dumb, maybe really dumb. But if public officials could only be taken seriously on the condition they never say anything dumb, no one would ever have credibility.

There are lessons in *The Emperor's New Clothes* if you're willing to look at it. Remember, *"A republic, if you can keep it."*

CHAPTER 10

The Press in the Trump Era

News – newly received or noteworthy information, especially about recent or important events.

ON FRIDAY, JULY 27, 2018 THE COMMERCE DEPARTMENT reported a 4.1 percent rate of growth in the U.S. economy in the second quarter. It was the strongest growth in nearly four years. This report came with the backdrop from the previous day of a remarkable deal, or the beginnings of a deal, that will put the U.S. and the European Union on good terms for trade agreements and possibly remove all tariffs by either the U.S. or the European Union – tariff neutral trading. The positive effects to the U.S. economy, to hard working people in both the U.S. and Europe, to economic survival on its way to prosperity, was the news that day!

The news that day was the strong rate of growth in the U.S. economy. Anderson Cooper of CNN didn't so much report it as he referred to it in the last minutes of his broadcast wrapped in a "good news/bad news" context without any reporting on even the basic details of the good economic news. He opened with his "Keeping Them Honest" segment about how everybody in the Trump sphere are liars relating to the Russian thing. He ran a series of clips edited to score some kind of "gotcha" point about Trump's bankrupt credibility. Cooper's sarcasm oozed throughout.

Cooper took up most all of the broadcast messaging with the lying by Trump and his people and Russia collusion. Cooper had Stormy Daniels' attorney Michael Avenatti on to discuss the Michael Cohen aspect of the Robert Mueller investigation. Avenatti was unnecessarily insulting and condescending to the other guest on that segment, Harvard law professor emeritus, Alan Dershowitz. It was hyperbolically infused sand box misbehavior on the part of Avenatti. It was wholly unimportant, taking-up valuable air time that could have been used to cover the relevant news of the day – the strong rate of growth in the U.S. economy.

The news that day was the strong rate of growth in the U.S. economy. Don Lemon of CNN didn't report it. Instead he announced "breaking news" and reported about Michael Cohen and the Robert Mueller investigation, the Trump Tower meeting with Russians, a Rudy Giuliani interview as Trump's attorney and the porn actress, Stormy Daniels. Throughout the broadcast there were panel discussions with a harmonic chorus of talking heads rehashing the aforementioned.

The news that day was the strong rate of growth in the U.S. economy. Ari Melber, sitting in for Rachel Maddow on her news show, didn't report it. He said it was a big news day, which it was because of the strong rate of growth in the U.S. economy, but he reported on Trump presiding over a National Security Council meeting on election security, Michael Cohen, Robert Mueller seen at an airport, the upcoming Paul Manafort trial, immigrant kids separated from parents.

The news that day was the strong rate of growth in the U.S. economy.

* * *

Despite the essential role of the press in our Republic, the press in its own right is not a noble profession. This may sound blasphemous, but no profession is noble in its own right. This includes teaching, medicine, the law, the clergy, politics, and everything else. Journalists, bad at their craft, often act as if because they're journalists they are high and mighty. Any critique of them, they feel, is against the First Amendment and against righteousness. Know this, dear reader: It's never the profession that ennobles. Rather, it's the practitioner that ennobles goodness, or on the other end of the spectrum, disgraces what should be good.

The Need of a Trustworthy Press

A trustworthy press in all its forms – print media, digital media, broadcast media, or skywriting for that matter – is essential and indispensible to our Republic. The previously mentioned news broadcasts of July 27, 2018 demonstrate that the First Amendment is alive and well. They also demonstrate that journalism, as a source of news, is dead. To be fair, journalism is dead at these particular outlets. But these outlets are still considered "mainstream." Meaning they are afforded some kind of widespread credibility. (Although maybe, hopefully, they will eventually lose such stature – as they deserve.) *Side note:* This is an example of a phenomenon where a word like "mainstream" is used so commonly the word no longer accurately describes what it is describing. I have a suspicion that the so-called "mainstream" media/news does not reflect mainstream American opinions and attitudes, and that the state of affairs are a lot more complicated than presented by the so-called "mainstream" media. In any case, in this era, I will call it "mainstream" to keep it simple.

In these still-considered "mainstream"-media outlets there is an army of so-called reporters, which include commentators and pundits, who are nothing less than disgraceful in their bad reporting, bad commentary, and bad punditry. The bad work they do and the disgrace of their reporting, commentary, and punditry is not a function of sharp differences of opinion that naturally occur across the political spectrum. I wish that were so. Rather, their work product is wholly disingenuous, lacking any degree of objectivity, context, or critical thinking. They work backward from the narrative they want and backfill with anything to falsely support their narrative. It's full-proof … unless you have brain. These journalists or opinion-journalists are at the least persons with impaired sensibility or at the worst persons with rabid pathology.

The Fourth Estate

Journalism is the activity or profession of writing newspapers, magazines, or news websites, or preparing news reports to be broadcast. Journalism is known as "the fourth estate." This term is significant due to its purpose and origins. The fourth estate, also known as "the fourth power," refers to a part of society that has formidable influence without being an institutional component of the political system. The term "fourth estate" comes from the historical European idea of a society divided into three segments: the clergy, the nobility, and the commoners. The fourth estate could be any influence that has the "ear" of power: lawyers, philosophers, the mistresses of kings, and so on.

The American version of this idea morphs the three segments of the old European concept, which also encompasses the principle of *separation of powers*, into the three branches of government: legislative, executive, and judiciary. Journalism, the press, colloquially became the "fourth branch of government." The terms "The fourth branch of government" and "the fourth estate" can be used interchangeably.

Journalism, as "the fourth power," is considered the fourth branch of our government. While journalistic opinion can run the gamut, as "the fourth power," journalism, if it seeks to maintain standards of credibility, has a unique and *moral obligation* to report all news *accurately*, *impartially*, and *truthfully*. In its efforts to control the public mind and will (something it's not supposed to do), the largest segment of the press – known as "mainstream" journalism – has not only abrogated its responsibility to the American people, it has abrogated its responsibility to our Republic.

As the fourth estate is now traditionally used to mean the press, it's interesting to note that "the fourth estate" also refers to "the mob," as in mob rule. It's easy to see how things in a society can get out of hand as a result of the press.

News – newly received or noteworthy information, especially about recent or important events.

It's "*a republic if you can keep it.*"

CHAPTER 11

Life Imitating Reality TV

YOU HAVE TO WONDER WHAT'S REAL, WHAT'S NOT, and what matters. Then after you're done wondering, you have to know and get it right. Today everything seems to be scripted, staged, and played out like a Greek tragedy with Orwellian overtones, *Twilight Zone* ironies and twists, Shakespearian lessons in human nature and thirst for power, roller derby pointlessness, and MSNBC assessment of what it all means.

Donald Trump is president of the United States of America. Prior to that he was a mega businessman. Already entrenched as a pop culture shinny object icon, he launched a popular and successful reality TV show with unknown contestants. He discovered the bitchiest bitch known to human kind. We loved watching her set herself up for a huge humiliating take down – Donald Trump pointed his finger like it was a pistol, aimed it between the eyes of the bitch Omarosa, and shot the words, "You're fired!" Sweet!

She should have been fired in an early episode for being a self-centered, self-righteous, incompetent bitch, but she was ratings gold.

Donald Trump and his producers brilliantly knew they had to keep her on long enough so the public could relish hating her until they could relish her defeat.

Donald Trump wasn't done. If *The Apprentice* was a shinny object, *Celebrity Apprentice* was shinier and sexier. And the bitch Omarosa, whom Donald Trump discovered and made a *faux* celebrity from nothing, cast her to do exactly what she did before, only better. It played out to the masses just the way we wanted it and probably needed it. Thank you, Donald Trump.

But wait, Donald Trump wasn't done. He got elected president of the United States of America ... hmm. He had another reality show trick up his sleeve. Let's bring the bitch Omarosa into the White House, into the Trump Administration, as a made-up top level advisor to the president (YOU CAN'T MAKE THIS STUFF UP). What could go wrong? Don't get ahead of me, because where I'm going nothing did go wrong. Stick with me.

Once in the White House, the bitch Omarosa immediately began plying her trade. She embarrassingly and excessively lauded Donald Trump. She showed how to "brown nose" at the highest level. The agenda-driven media mistakenly thinks Donald Trump loves this. He could hardly care; he looked the other way. After all he was busy being president.

Predictably, the bitch Omarosa made her presence known in the most petty ways. She abused her use of the White House car service for her own personal needs. She had some kind of job that no one really understood what it was. And, apparently she didn't even do it. She bullied people and barred African-Americans access to the White House because she wanted to be the top African-American of those who were already there. With her sense of self-importance and no, or uncertain, authorization she stormed the White House grounds with her large wedding party for a photo shoot before she was told by security police to get the hell out and take her party with her.

(Just so you don't think I'm too heavy-handed as I've been calling her "the bitch Omarosa," let me point out the bitch Omarosa refers to herself that way in the book she authored, *The Bitch Switch: Knowing How to Turn It on and Off*. I guess I don't know how to turn it off.)

Donald Trump, ever the world-class chess player on world affairs and the open air ice rink in Central Park, author of *The Art of the Deal* (who cares whether or not he wrote it?), showed his detractors, as if to say, "Hey, idiots, you think a reality TV star can't run the country? I can bring the show right into the White House to give you, the fake news, enough 'red meat' to choke on, and still do a much better job than anyone from the swamp has ever done."

So, the stage was set. Everyone knew when the bitch Omarosa was fired by White House Chief of Staff, General John Kelly, she was going to come out with a tell-all/tell-nothing book that would be self-serving with the most unverified, damning items about Trump. It would be dripping with disgusting assertions and innuendo.

The agenda-driven press, even though they collectively viewed the bitch Omarosa with contempt and as having no credibility, allowed her to make the rounds on all the fake news outlets. For them it didn't matter if she vomited egregious lies. No matter the utter lack of credibility, the sound of it was still music to their ears. Their own duplicity was lost on them — another example of the fakeness that goes into their fake news.

So, we have the bitch Omarosa perfectly teed-up in all her glory. I feel like if I were a host on a TV talk show with a studio audience and I had the bitch Omarosa on as a guest and we watched a video compilation of the bitch Omarosa's betrayal tour to this point, and Donald Trump then walked on stage, stood silently stone-faced, I would, in the manner of Jack Benny, turn my head in the direction of the audience, and tilt my head slightly to convey calmly, without speaking a word, what is now going to unfold without inhibition or restraint between these two titans of "not letting it go."

For those who are young and don't know the Jack Benny reference, I'm sorry, I couldn't resist. Go to the Internet to look at old video footage. Benny had a great deadpan. It'll be good for you.

OK, getting back to the action. Donald Trump requires a worthy opponent. Kim Jong Un and Vladimir Putin have nothing compared to the bitch Omarosa. Even their names are whimpy. Un, that's not a name it's a noise. Putin, sounds a little like putz. The bitch Omarosa, now there's a name. And, she has the temperament, low character, and street cred to do the throw down with Donald Trump. So, the most powerful person in the world, Donald Trump, and the bitch Omarosa, the villain of all villains, a Trump creation, were now in a rhetorical death match. It's brilliant! High stakes, low brow entertainment for the masses. Bring the kids, after all their innocence was blown generations ago.

When things happen, you have to know what's real and what the moral of the story is. For the agenda-driven press, the moral of the story is Stormy Daniels and if Trump ever used the "n" word. Gotcha Trump! For everyone who knows what's real and knows what's going on, the moral of the story is – since Trump took office as president, unemployment for everyone, particularly minorities, has been at record lows.

PART III

WHO'S CRAZY?

MY OBJECTIVE IN WRITING THIS BOOK IS TO AWAKEN readers to the dangers from ignorance of issues effecting public policy and to elevate their understanding of people and the societal/ governmental dynamics of our Republic in order to equip them for the weighty task of *if you can keep it*. If you've been reading this book and have gotten to this point because I've held your interest and you were willing to spend your time with my ideas, I hope my objective is being realized.

* * *

The matter of mental instability is unavoidable if you want to take on the prevailing winds of cultural and political discourse. In Part III of this book, I lay out an essential discussion of mental illness – its legitimate consideration and its unethical, ridiculous misuse for political attacks.

In consideration of mental health issues, it's necessary to provide sound perspectives on societal, clinical, and psychological dynamics. There's no way to convey what is at stake for our society without correctly assessing the demands of this Republic and the current political climate and its threat to good governance without people's sufficient understanding of who's crazy.

I'm not just taking a swipe at an opposing view. The forces against sensibility and intellectual integrity are formidable and without regard for the destruction of principles that keep our Republic alive. Even before Trump was elected, anti-Trump media seriously discussed the 25th Amendment to the *Constitution* as a reasonable remedy to remove Trump from office should he win the election.

The 25th Amendment is a provision to replace the president or vice president in the event of death, resignation, or incapacitation. Section 4 of the Amendment is the bullet. It addresses incapacitation, which includes mental disturbance rendering a person unfit for the office. So, if you think the president is nuts and you're the VP, a cabinet member, or a congressional designate, you can make a fuss to have the president removed. And, oh yes, to remove a president this way it would and should be necessary to clinically prove that he or she *is* nuts.

The anti-Trump media must have thought they had a slam dunk with this remedy. They surely wouldn't waste the thoughtful public's time if it wasn't obvious Trump is certifiably off his rocker.

* * *

Throw Down

In October, 2017 *The Dangerous Case of Donald Trump* was published. It's a compilation of essays/chapters on various aspects of Donald Trump's "psychopathology." It has twenty-seven academic clinical experts as contributors. The book's cover identifies Bandy Lee, M.D., M.Div., as the primary author and Organizer of the Yale "Duty to Warn" Conference.

In the book's Prologue, Judith Lewis Herman and Bandy X. Lee write:

> *When we circulated our letters of concern, we asked our fellow mental health professionals to get involved in politics not only as citizens (a right most of us still enjoy) but also, specifically, as professionals and as guardians of the special knowledge with which they have been entrusted. Why do we think this was permissible? It is all too easy to claim, as we did, that an emergency situation requires a departure from our usual practices in the private sphere. How can one judge whether political involvement is in fact justified?*

"… as professionals and as *guardians of the special* knowledge with which they have been entrusted." Wow, if you believed this you'd think their book was ordained by the highest authority of the universe as the most sacred mission ever.

This is a high-profile collection of prestigious expert/authors, associated with an honored Ivy League institution, laying out an all-in, unequivocal throw down, sound-the-alarm alert to the "psychopathology" of Donald Trump. The term "duty to warn" has an unmistakable meaning in the field of mental health – it mandates authoritative action. A duty to warn is based on the determination an individual is a danger to him- or herself and/or others.

You can't get any more expert and authoritative than Dr. Lee and her expansive team of clinical experts. So, why hasn't a psychiatric emergency team visited the White House, assessed President Trump, and taken him to a psychiatric hospital for a 72-hour hold? Because it would be ridiculous! The premise of Dr. Lee's book lacks purposeful integrity. It's not about a properly conducted assessment of Trump's psychological functioning. The book's contributors are not only wrong in their collective assessment, they have all violated professional ethics. The book is a political "hatchet job."

During the campaign for the 1964 presidential election a magazine published an article in which psychiatrists who hadn't examined candidate Barry Goldwater were polled on his fitness to be president. Goldwater sued the magazine for libel and won. He was awarded $75,000 in damages.

The American Psychiatric Association (APA) subsequently established a rule which appeared in the first edition of the APA's *Principles of Medical Ethics* in 1973. It was informally called the Goldwater rule. The rule is in section 7 of this ethics manual. It reads:

> *On occasion psychiatrists are asked for an opinion about an individual who is in the light of public attention or who has disclosed information about himself/herself through public media. In such circumstances, a psychiatrist may share with the public his or her expertise about psychiatric issues in general. However, it is unethical for a psychiatrist to offer a professional opinion unless he or she has conducted an examination and has been granted proper authorization for such a statement.*

The Lee book's prologue makes a lame argument as to why publishing the book is a justified violation of the Goldwater rule. Their argument is fraught with defect and absurdity.

There wouldn't be any problem if all the experts from the "Lee team" thought Trump was horrible as president and unfit to hold the office. They could say he's a jerk and an idiot as well as an embarrassment to this country. They can despise his policies and his governance. They can call for his impeachment. They have a right to their opinions as regular people. But in the name of the mental health profession these esteemed experts cross a line that actually causes real danger rather than the nonexistent danger they are warning about. They are abusing a sacred responsibility that comes when the designation of expert has been conferred on persons by societal authorization.

What do these "experts" say about Maxine Waters, Adam Schiff, Harry Reid, Richard Blumenthal, Kirsten Gillibrand, Nancy Pelosi, Jeff Flake, Al Franken, Mazie Hirono, Roy Moore, Sheila Jackson Lee, Joe Arpaio, and so on? And in the media arena, what do they say about Kathy Griffin, Rosie O'Donnell, Lawrence O'Donnell, Joe Scarborough, Alex Jones, Joy Behar, Steve Bannon, Michael Moore, and so on? And in the public administration arena, what do they say about James Comey, Andrew McCabe, Peter Strozk, John Koskinen, Lois Lerner, and so on?

The point is there's no end to the people in public life who have immense authority and influence in our culture and society who are imbalanced, extreme, and a threat to sensibility and decency. Many are crazy, off-the-rails crackpots. This includes mental health professionals who, blinded by passions and subject to fits of crazy, disregard the ethics of their profession.

* * *

In this Republic of governance, we have the principle of *checks and balances*. Just as in governance, *checks and balances* are essential in public discourse. The idea Trump is unhinged and mentally disturbed and as such dangerous is popular and widespread. But we are, have been, and will likely continue to be a polarized nation. Just as popular and widespread (which includes esteemed experts) is the idea Trump not only poses no threat due to mental instability, he brings exactly the right corrections and stabilizations to governance and policy for this nation to be well and thrive.

Being a polarized nation has been viewed as problematic – when political forces tear the people apart, it's understandable why polarization is seen as bad. In the current climate, leftists, who are solidly anti-Trump, are obsessed with the extinction of different ideas, causing our current polarization. It would be good to under-stand polarization differently, and accept the reality of differences in thinking. The free market of ideas is where we get *checks and balances* on public discourse. It is where the most polarized positions can be debated, discussed, and possibly resolved along a continuum of better understanding. This, however, can only be done if rhetorical low-blows such as ad hominem attacks – calling a political opponent a racist or mentally disturbed – are eliminated from the discourse. Representative government democratically chosen (elected), the First Amendment, *and* the free market for ideas are the components of preserving our Republic.

Professional Wrestling

The analogy of professional wrestling serves to illustrate how we have currently allowed a breakdown of First Amendment principles – which corrupts the Republic and threatens its existence. Remember, it's "*a republic, if you can keep it.*"

Professional wrestling (fake sport) is really a morality play with a very specific and profoundly good purpose. It's a warning to all of us not to be fooled by foolishness. The wrestling ring is the stage. It has firm identifiable boundaries. There is a match contested by two unambiguous opponents – a bad guy, thoroughly evil, and a good guy, a champion of what is right and just. The match is governed by firm, identifiable rules.

So, as always, the stage is set for how the match is to be conducted. What actually plays out is a violation of every wrestling-match rule (and sensibility) with the outcome choreographed and predetermined. No matter how the contestants perform, the match is wholly rigged. The bad guy runs out of the ring; that should mean he loses right there. When out of the ring, he grabs a folding chair, comes back into the ring with the chair folded, and smashes it over the head of the good guy! Really? Not only should he lose the match, the police should be called to arrest this sociopath for assault with a deadly weapon. The referee, the guy who's supposed to see to it the rules are followed, the adult in the room, who's getting paid good money, is nowhere to be found. Oh, he's physically there, but he's looking the other way, or letting it go, or waving his arms signaling his disapproval, and demonstrating his impotence.

The way professional wrestling is performed is exactly how our current discourse of ideas, policies, identity politics, and values are played out. We are a cartoon version of professional wrestling. We can only see things as virtuous or evil, stable or crazy. What's worse is over time, and it doesn't take long, we become the cartoon characters we despise. The Lee team, their book, and their *Duty to Warn* conference plays right into the cartoon-character roles the morality play of professional wrestling warns against. Honest, intelligent discourse is silenced. With the diagnosis of psychopathology rendered by the Lee team "experts," it's easy not to have to discuss any of the controversial issues that will always face society. We don't need to hear Trump; he's crazy. We don't need to hear people who voted for him; they're crazy too.

Crossed a Line

As I said, these "experts" crossed a line. If these "guardians of the special knowledge" were truly worried that Trump's mental condition was a danger to himself and us, they would not, and should not go public with it. There are proper, discrete channels for processing legitimate mental health concerns. These "experts" not only violated what little privacy Trump can savor, with the help of a complicit media, they created a bigger danger by stoking unfounded concern in a huge segment of already over-the-top hysterical people. Moreover, when a licensed clinician does go through the proper channels to register mental health dangers, they need to *get it right!* – and not allow personal politics to drive the assessment.

As previously noted, the overall assessment rendered by the Dr. Lee team should have triggered the legal mandate to notify the psychiatric emergency team. Despite their absolute conviction of the *danger* involved (it's in the book's title), the Lee team failed to notify the mental health authorities. Well, the Lee team didn't notify the local psychiatric authorities because if the emergency team showed up to field test and assess Trump for dangerous mental instability based on the case to which these "esteemed experts" devoted an entire book, the emergency team would have laughed their asses off at the absurdity and baselessness of the warning call. And the Lee team knows it.

The Lee team crossed the line because however extreme and oddball they find Trump, clinically and professionally, they *got it wrong*. Their book outlined a patchwork of misapplied observations, speculations, and self-righteous moralizing. From such, they collectively rendered a hostile and abusive clinical assessment. The work was politically motivated … shame on them.

So, to answer the question – who's crazy? – *Anyone who can't be sensible when it's necessary.*

CHAPTER 12

Two Assessments of Mental Status

I'M AN EXPERT IN PSYCHOLOGICAL EVALUATION. I WRITE detailed reports on psychological functioning. My reports have been used in courts of law to make just rulings in cases that have serious consequences for those whom it affects. I have a track record in which my recommendations based on my assessment reports have prevailed 100 percent in court rulings.

Reports of psychological functioning must meet exacting standards. As precise as these reports are, there is also an art to the assessment process and the production of the report. An essential feature of an evaluation is what is known as the "Mental Status Exam." In this chapter, I'm going to render a mental status exam (with occasional commentary) on the public profile of Donald Trump.

Now, let's deal with the legal and ethical matters of publishing my assessment as an expert on what would be confidential information relating to a patient in my private practice. Donald Trump is not my patient. While he is entitled to privacy regarding clinical matters, he is a public figure, allowing some latitude for me as an expert to discuss him from a public perspective. Also, note that I specified an exam (with occasional commentary) on "the public profile of Donald Trump." This is an assessment of his public profile, not his personal and private clinical condition – an important and critical distinction. Let's proceed.

Mental Status, Donald Trump

Donald Trump is a 72 year-old male who presents with a forward manner and a firm handshake sometimes to the point where he holds his grip and pulls you close to him. This gesture has been often viewed by media personalities as inappropriately aggressive. In the full context of his personality and self-awareness, together with confidence and strength he wants to project when he meets people, it can also convey something more friendly and open. He is fully aware of his stature and celebrity in this society and the world at large. He is quite friendly and personable. Reciprocal friendliness is important to him.

Mr. Trump is physically active and animated. He gestures with one or both hands to accentuate what he is saying. His hand gestures are idiosyncratic and widely recognized as his characteristic mannerism.

Mr. Trump is well-groomed and sports a distinctive hair style. He acknowledges his signature look, understanding it's perpetually the target of jokes, often to the point of mockery and ridicule. He gets much attention just for his stylized look. He takes this attention in a good-natured way, indicating a strength and confidence in himself and how he presents. Mr. Trump usually dresses in well-tailored business suits, always dark charcoal grey, always a white dress shirt with a tie that is solid color or diagonally stripped. This attire is also part of his signature look.

Mr. Trump is tall and somewhat overweight compared to his younger years. He has a good appetite and enjoys food, including desserts. And with regard to enjoyment, he relishes being in control of large scale enterprises without limits. He thinks well of himself and his abilities. He likes to be the center of attention. However, his intense drive to be in charge does not override his respect for individual integrity, skill, and independence in others. He demands much from others in his association, including loyalty.

To his ardent opponents Mr. Trump has a reputation for constantly telling lies. Context is necessary to understand this trait and how it functions in his life. Lying is something that most people do for many reasons. In his extreme hyper-political world, everything he says, every word he speaks is reflexively, severely, and aggressively attacked by the highest of profile people. From political opponents to journalist pundits to media celebrities, Mr. Trump is never afforded any benefit of doubt that his ideas, decisions, and policies are well-thought out and motivated for doing the best for the most people, as well as respecting the rights of all.

Mr. Trump purposely and mindfully injected himself into this "take no prisoners" world public arena of hateful-enemy political opposition in the extreme. His opponents have no boundaries when it comes to lying. He could legitimately say the collection of his opponents have no rival in terms of lying. Mr. Trump, acknowledged as a "counter puncher" to his opposition, routinely and effectively turns the tables by branding his opponents as liars. An example is calling oppositional propaganda news "fake news."

Again, context is essential to understanding how Mr. Trump chooses to deal with oppositional challenges. The analogy of a gladiatorial competitor does not overstate the dynamics involved. Politics, often referred to as a "blood sport," indicates what a hardened, but accurate, view can be had about the "war" of politics, particularly presidential politics. Even if one finds it distasteful and disapproves as they would in a gladiator's battle to the death, lying is a ubiquitous tool in the political arena.

Mr. Trump sets his sights on big, historic accomplishments to bring about benefits for all. He is, however, realistic about timing, motivation, and obstacles. "We've done very well in our negotiation with China, but we're not prepared to make the deal that they'd like to make. We'll continue to talk to China." He has a strategic sense of balance between urgency and patience.

Mr. Trump does not get hung up over details unless he wants to clarify and/or defend a point. It's noteworthy when he does take the time to explain complicated things in detail, he demonstrates his keen grasp of knowledge and comprehension.

Although not formally tested in this assessment, Mr. Trump evidences at least above average intelligence with keen sensibilities about business, construction, system operations, political instincts, judgment of others, and communication. He tends to speak in generalities. He is not articulate in the sense of having a mature, professional sound in word choice and speaking pattern. He speaks plainly and in simple terms, regularly using superlatives to describe people and things – "terrific," "amazing," "the best," "the greatest," "very very," "incredible," "tremendous," and so on. Certainly the common use of such words is not remarkable in itself, but what is distinctive is the regular pattern and cadence of Mr. Trump's language and speech. This is so well-recognized as his public persona it is a much impersonated characteristic on the worldwide stage of entertainment and beyond.

Another aspect of Mr. Trump's style of speech, together with what was previously described, is he usually talks in a way that is "off-the-cuff," unguarded, and not articulate. When he reads prepared speeches, Mr. Trump demonstrates a genuine connection with the message. As such speeches are carefully scripted, his articulation increases to a high level with sophisticated, profound, and thoughtful ideation. He does not want his ideas or other ideas he agrees with to be only academic. Even when he reads a prepared speech, Mr. Trump often interrupts himself and goes off script to provide spontaneous commentary in the style of simple statements just noted. This is an indication of how he personalizes ideas.

In regard to his public speaking in any manner or other communication format such as Twitter, Mr. Trump demonstrates unusual bluntness any time he speaks or messages. In this way he is undeterred by the large and hostile part of the public, together with a majority of the press, in aggressive opposition to him. He is verbally, or in writing, attacked personally for almost anything he says. Despite such formidable intellectual aggression and hostility against him, Mr. Trump is unrestrained to do what he thinks is correct. It should be noted, there are at least or as near as many of the public who agree with Mr. Trump's positions as those who disagree, and are against him.

Mr. Trump is fully-aware of what he does and the choices he makes. He is well-aware and oriented to not only his physical surroundings but where he is situated with others, at large, and their orientation to him. He feels he has thoughtful justification for his words and actions, which is observable from a profile assessment perspective whether or not one agrees with his general reasoning.

With ease and no hesitation, Mr. Trump can poke fun at himself. He claims not to use recreational drugs or drink alcohol. "I've never had alcohol." He added, self-deprecatingly, "Can you imagine if I had? ... What a mess I'd be? ... I'd be the world's worst!"

Mr. Trump likes to engage with people. He shares his thoughts and feelings openly. He is readily accessible; he is intellectually and emotionally unguarded. He demonstrates an understanding of human nature and organizes his thinking in accordance with relevance and priorities.

Mr. Trump has little or no tolerance for persons he considers fools. He usually does not refrain from expressing his low opinion of others. He is critical and given to ridiculing and/or making fun of such people. Mr. Trump does not sugarcoat his disapprovals and is no-nonsense when it comes to things he doesn't like.

Mr. Trump discriminates between those whom he considers negatively and those he regards well and respects. He also demonstrates great capacity for compassion, recognizing the challenges and hardship's suffered by people. On more than a few occasions where previous administrations failed, Mr. Trump had his administration successfully intercede to release political prisoners from totalitarian regimes without making concessions or paying ransom in any form.

Also notable is Mr. Trump's pattern of pardons for persons convicted of crimes. Presidents in the past signed pardons on their last day in office to avoid political fallout for pardons viewed as corrupt and improper by political opponents. Mr. Trump has signed pardons in a manner suggesting he makes his decisions, for better or worse, without playing politics. He does this in the "light of day," no doubt pleased to get approval for his decisions, but willing to take criticism as well. Whether one is in agreement with Mr. Trump's decisions, this speaks to his integrity as it relates to his character in this regard.

Mr. Trump is a strong personality standout. He may even be considered unusual. But from a mental status perspective, Mr. Trump is alert and well-oriented to his physical and situational surroundings. He is able to focus his attention as needed. He works well in extreme and demanding circumstances. There is no bizarre ideation, tangentiality, or thought disturbance. Cognitive functioning is intact. There is no delusional or irrational thinking. He evidences no character disorder, psychopathology, or personality disorder. Mr. Trump is strongly opinionated and action oriented. He demonstrates a robust ego strength. His mental status is stable.

* * *

Well, that was interesting. For perspective, I'll render another mental status exam (with occasional commentary).

Let's profile a composite persona reflecting an amalgam of personalities in the mainstream media. This segment of societal culture and influence is overwhelmingly anti-Trump. In the same way an individual can be assessed in terms of mental status, so too can this persona-amalgam be assessed from a public profile perspective. Let's call this composite persona "Mr. Oppotrumpmedia." This stands for opposition-to-Trump-media. And, forgive me, if you must, for choosing the masculine designation for our composite representative, which does include males and females as well as other diversities. It could be feminine or gender-nonspecific. I simply want to use a traditional formal name prefix and associated pronouns (Mr., he, his, him). Let's proceed.

Mental Status, Mr. Oppotrumpmedia

Mr. Oppotrumpmedia is an influencer who's age ranges from about thirty to seventy years old (remember, a composite person). In some way, he is as old as all the collective institutions informing public opinion in any culture and society.

In this era, at this time and place, the most prominent thing that stands out about Mr. Oppotrumpmedia is his extreme resentment and bitterness. He has a very high opinion of himself with the expectation that his self-opinion should be unquestionably shared by the public at large. "… will the country stand up for them (referring to people without a voice, figuratively) … We the decent, truly patriotic people who really love America and believe in its greatness have to." Anyone or any segment of the public not having a high regard for Mr. Oppotrumpmedia, he feels, must have something characterologically and morally wrong with them. The resentment and bitterness harbored by Mr. Oppotrumpmedia was triggered by the presidential election of 2016 when Donald Trump was elected in accordance to the Constitutional provision of the Electoral College by a surprisingly wide margin.

Mr. Oppotrumpmedia is well-dressed in business suit attire, well-groomed, articulate, and well-spoken with excellent communication skills. He has very good camera presence for television broadcast. Despite his contempt for Trump, he has an ironically symbiotic relationship with Trump, as Mr. Oppotrumpmedia owes his viewing audience to seeing him trash Trump 24/7 (all the time, it never ends).

Mr. Oppotrumpmedia's daily commentary is solely based on his narrowly and repeatedly filtered premise of Trump being a liar and a racist: "This president traffics in racism." "He continues repeating the same lies," He routinely evokes Trump's words and rhetoric as a "dog whistle" conveying to an imagined racist-disturbed political base Trump's "real" sick beliefs. Mr. Oppotumpmedia's passionate and obsessive contempt for Trump eclipses any argument to give reason for his contempt. If Trump does anything objectively positive, Mr. Opotrumpmedia minimizes, dismisses, misrepresents it as not positive, or ignores it altogether.

Mr. Oppotrumpmedia is subject to hysterical outbursts of invectives and irrationality. He draws illogical conclusions and makes unsubstantiated negative attributions about Trump. " ... you crazy lunatic 70 year-old man/baby, stop it! You are now the President of the United States, the Commander in Chief, and you need to stop acting like a mean girl!! ... we won't work with you!"

Mr. Oppotrumpmedia willfully expends energy to criticize and discredit Trump. Due to many of Trump's objective achievements, it is likely that Mr. Oppotrumpmedia is in some way aware Trump's appeal and approval is growing among the mainstream electorate. This causes a reaction formation in Mr. Oppotrumpmedia. Due to his commitment to "Trump contempt," he experiences a cognitive and emotional crisis if he acknowledges anything decent, good, or normal about Trump. The word "normal" as it could relate to Trump is concerning to Mr.Oppotrumpmedia. He often displays the need to oppose anything that would *normalize* Trump.

Shakespeare wrote, "The lady doth protest too much" to convey that in human nature if you lay it on too thick it's hard to believe. In such a way, Mr. Oppotrumpmedia has invested so much emotional energy enabling the anti-Trump cause, he has to see Trump in extremes, no matter how ridiculous, or admit to himself how wrong he has been. Mr. Oppotrumpmedia is in a constant state of ego collapse as he strains believability to himself. He can't allow himself to say something like, "Trump maybe an OK guy even if I don't like him a lot or really disagree with him."

Projective identification is a defense mechanism and coping tactic Mr. Oppotrumpmedia has emotionally formulated to manage the reality of Trump. He sees bad things in Trump stemming from undesirable thoughts and feelings Mr. Oppotrumpmedia has about himself, of which he may be unaware. These coping and defense mechanisms are an effort to rationalize and endure what is intolerable to him: Trump is the president ... Trump exists.

The immediate world in which Mr. Oppotrumpmedia surrounds himself contributes and nourishes his mental status. His engagements in his media work are almost exclusively with people in the media who are aligned with his worldview, particularly his politics.

Every day/evening on his broadcast, Mr. Oppotrumpmedia has panel discussions, sometimes large panels, loaded with what seems like 90-percent or more panel contributors who are carbon copies of one another's anti-Trump vitriol – some of whom work themselves up to a rhetorical frenzy. This creates a self-validating echo chamber, subjecting the panel to group hysteria. Any dissenting view and commentary offered by a panel member with different views is dismissively shut down and marginalized. These dissenters, usually in a polite manner, show deference to the others. As such, opportunities are wasted to challenge even the "low hanging fruit" of illogic, irrationality, and flaws in the views of Mr. Oppotrumpmedia and the panel at large.

From a checks-and-balance perspective to foster critical analytics for more reliable comprehension of things, these conditions for Mr. Oppotrumpmedia are particularly disabling, given his profession. Journalism and punditry, at their best, are based on sound analytical reasoning. Mr. Oppotrumpmedia has either purposely or obliviously shut-off any "tests of reliability" required for credible analysis and credibility in general.

Mr. Oppotrumpmedia's audience can be profiled into three segments: (1) passive viewers who consider these broadcast networks mainstream default ideology, (2) devoted adherents to the networks' packaged ideology, and (3) a large portion of viewers who monitor anti-Trump media to stay updated as to what they're up against. Putting aside the serious implications to our Republic, this last group may enjoy as an amusement the absurdity they find in the anti-Trump media, which to them seems to outdo itself every day. "… this president thinks that law enforcement should not be independent and should answer to him and should serve his purposes." With such commentary, Mr. Oppotrumpmedia displays some paranoia.

In the same way a politician has a political base, Mr. Oppotrumpmedia and the anti-Trump media he belongs to also has an audience/political base. His punditry/journalism is a product to serve his base. This is an additional reinforcement of who he is, how he functions, and his worldview. An additional reinforcement is the substantial monetary compensation he gets, although it's likely he would hold these views without the financial imbursement; but it's sure a nice perk.

Mr. Oppotrumpmedia is particularly sensitive to criticism of himself and the media he champions. There is an arrogance in his attitude that conveys the media, particularly the press, are above criticism. He thinks he and they are untouchable, as if the First Amendment means "don't speak against the press." Mr. Oppotrumpmedia fails to understand the First Amendment really means "have at it." Mr. Oppotrumpmedia fails to understand that in our Republic we have freedom of speech all the way around. And "may the best speech win." Mr. Oppotrumpmedia fails to understand, or accept, although he disagrees with Trump, that maybe Trump's speech is better and more convincing than the speech he himself likes.

Mr. Oppotrumpmedia demonstrates concrete thinking and reasoning about almost everything. For any well-oriented and stable person, in the course of engaging with people, a critical stabilizing function of apprehension and comprehension is to nimbly gauge what is said and what is meant. It's like a car's shock-absorber system – shock-absorbers allow a car to drive smoothly over a bumpy road surface. The passenger doesn't want to experience every bump. Bumps aren't the reason they're in a car. They're in a car because they're going somewhere. With concrete thinking, what happens is – they experience every "bump" and focus on its distraction, and lose sight of the meaning – where they're supposed to go.

In his commentary, Mr. Oppotrumpmedia processes and breaks down the public and, a few notable times, private communications of Trump and his surrogates. Mr. Oppotrumpmedia either fails to apprehend intended meanings or purposely twists meaning to suit his desired narrative. He routinely cites Trump's assertion about the Charlottesville demonstrations in August of 2017 that turned deadly. Trump said at a news conference, "… there's blame on both sides …. you also had people that were very fine people, on both sides." Mr. Oppotrumpmedia took Trump's comment (deliberately distorted) to mean Trump is a white supremacist. By "both sides" Trump was referring to the debate about the controversy over Civil War statues of Southern figures. Mr.Oppotrumpmedia said, "Cross burnings are tiki torches. Their white hoods replaced by no hoods and khaki pants. These are the very fine people in the President's eyes." It was clear in that press conference Trump appropriately and not surprisingly condemned those very neo-Nazis and white nationalist demonstrators. It was clear Trump did not think these were very fine people. In this regard, aided by concrete thinking, Mr. Oppotrumpmedia evidences a deficit in comprehension and reasoning, or a deficit in character, or a deficit in both.

Mr. Oppotrumpmedia states *the press is speaking truth to power*. Which is fine and as it should be as a First Amendment right. What he doesn't acknowledge is *power speaking truth to the press*, also afforded by the First Amendment. And as for "truth," Trump's criticisms are based on his assertion the truth is often absent in the press. He has labeled, branded, this press as "fake news." This infuriates Mr. Oppotrumpmedia.

But there's more. As a result of Mr. Oppotrumpmedia's rigid concreteness, he fails to see citing Trump's words are not enough to tell the full measure and significance of a news event or Trump's position. In this regard, news reporting and commenting are rendered fake, and hence, the reporters and commentators "enemies." Mr. Oppotrumpmedia is particularly indignant about the word "enemy" being applied to him. But disingenuous, fake news is an enemy of reason, and thus, the bearer of fake news is an enemy of our Republic.

Whether questioning Trump or his surrogates at news conferences, conducting interviews, giving commentary, or having panel discussions Mr. Oppotrumpmedia's concrete thinking and reasoning are the mechanisms by which he maintains a self-fulfilling, predetermined, purposeful narrative. Curiosity, thinking beyond this – his own narrative – is nonexistent. Concrete thinking is a serious barrier to logic and full comprehension. The daily press conference held by the press secretary is routinely contentious, often verbally hostile. This contentiousness is driven by journalists who are locked into concrete thinking, which is reflected in their indignant attitudes and questions.

Although not formally tested in this assessment, Mr. Oppotrumpmedia evidences intellectual functioning as high as the superior range. He likes to make a good impression and be seen favorably by others. He is usually polite, friendly, and courteous, although he can instantly turn contentious and dismissive.

He is alert and well-oriented to time and place. Cognition is intact. There is no bizarre ideation, tangentiality, or thought disturbance. Mental status is usually stable, but due to obsessional disappointment over the result of the 2016 presidential election and specifically for the contempt he derives from symbolic negative archetypes he infuses into Trump, *Mr. Oppotrumpmedia is vulnerable to a complete mental breakdown.*

This emotional vulnerability encompasses anger, anxiety, paranoia, and depression. To avert any further ill effects and reverse his mental and psychological course toward well-being it is strongly recommended Mr. Oppotrumpmedia avail himself of the services of a competent and trusted mental health specialist for psychotherapeutic counseling. It's further recommended the treating specialist be free from Trump derangement. There is a cost, however, if Mr. Oppotrumpmedia gets better: he will lose his job, his colleagues, and his friends.

* * *

That was also interesting. Mr. Oppotrumpmedia would probably take issue with this assessment. I would be pleased to sit down with him, or anyone who identifies with him, to show how this assessment, as all assessments, are reasoned. These assessments follow a standard. They are based on critical observation, context, and sensibility. An assessment is meant to describe and explain mental status. It is not meant to be a political statement or take a political position.

* * *

As far as mental status is concerned, ironically, Hillary Clinton may have identified more accurately in a general way the aspect of Trump's outward personality and characteristics. While many others, including experts, say Trump has psychopathology or a personality disorder, Hillary correctly called it his *temperament*. She repeatedly said, I'm paraphrasing, Trump has the wrong temperament to be President. You can debate whether you agree with that, but she rightly identified it as temperament, not pathology.

If you think Trump's a bad president, it's not because he's crazy. It should be noted, however, as of October 19, 2018, according to Politico/Morning Consult poll, most Americans think Trump is doing a good job as president.

By all evidence Trump is of sound mind. But he is quite a character. And news flash, being president is hazardous work for anyone. The anti-Trump media doesn't help. From a mental status perspective, whether you approve of him or not, Trump seems to be handling it quite well.

CHAPTER 13

Political Psychosis Derangement and Other Afflictions

I N THIS BOOK'S INTRODUCTION, I SAID I DIDN'T WANT TO GET too psycho-theoretically wonky. That was then, this is now. In this chapter I'm going to get very psycho-clinically-diagnostically wonky. Don't worry I'll walk you through carefully. After all, you've gotten this far, you'll be fine. So, put on your "wonky hat," … here we go.

Let's start with a few definitions of terms as they appear in this chapter:

Psychosis – Severe mental disorder in which thought and emotions are impaired. Contact with external reality is lost. (The title of this book – *A Loose Grip* – has a double meaning. One of the meanings relates to our "grip" on reality which is threatened by mental instability.)

Derangement – A disturbance in otherwise normal, healthy mental activity. There are erratic, irrational, and delusional thought processes causing psychological and emotional distress.

Agitation and impulsiveness can occur, worsening the distress. There is a disturbance in comprehension of the immediate interpersonal environment, as well as the world at large.

Hysteria – A psychological disorder characterized by irrational emotion and heightened concern about the threat of non-threatening things. Unwarranted emotional agitation. Hysteria can be confined to an individual or manifest in a group of infinite size (mass hysteria).

Anxiety – State of excessive tension and worry. Emotional distress characterized by inordinate nervousness, fear, and apprehension. Anxiety can have serious negative effects on rationality and functionality.

Delusion – Typically a symptom of a mental disorder where there is a firm belief in something that is demonstrably not real. Delusion usually plays a role in falsely supporting a complex of psychological and cognitive (processes in thinking) maladjustment.

Distress – Extreme negative pressure causing psychological, mental, and emotional anguish and suffering.

Dysfunction – Impairment and breakdown of essential mental operation. There is flawed and inadequate function negatively affecting well-being and normal sustainability in living.

Disordered Ideation – Thought confusion, lack of intellectual clarity, and illogical sensitivity. Thinking is disorganized or irrationally organized. Unreasonable and maladapted thought processes.

Syndrome – A combination of symptoms, signs, or characteristics that together define a disease or disorder – a clinical condition.

Paranoia – Mental condition characterized by delusions of persecution. An unfounded and irrational obsession that someone or something is committed and acting to do harm.

Non-disordered – A range of emotions and thought that is extreme but rational and understandable. Despite such extreme feelings there is an absence of psychological impairment and disturbance.

The Buzz Word – *Derangement*

In the public verbal "food fight," in the *pop/political arena*, one of the "word bullets" has been, and continues to be, "derangement." It's a good word, and a good "bullet." Even though you surely know what *derangement* means, I'm going to tell you what *derangement* means (you know what it means and you just read the definition above). But I'm going to tell you what *derangement* means by telling you where it "lives" amongst its "fellow gremlins" of psychological misfortune.

Remember, we're on our way through the psycho-clinical-diagnostic wonk "jungle" of *pop/political culture*. Here is the pathway:

General Precursors

The occurrence of certain general precursors creates fertile ground for collective hysteria and other political psychoses. All that is needed is a pervasive agenda-driven media to "water" this fertile ground. From there, hysteria takes root and grows. There are a variety of general precursors for hysteria, as well as for anxiety, delusions, and derangement. Here are just three types of precursors to give you an idea what a general precursor to political psychosis looks like:

Precursor 1: Quiet Desperation

In the well known quote from Henry David Thoreau, "The mass of men lead lives of quiet desperation." Thoreau observed and believed there was a psychological phenomenon common to most people, maybe in some way universal to all – the resignation toward life as unfulfilling. This state of mind/resignation would be the basis for a type of general precursor – susceptibility to emotional distresses and disturbed feelings. However, Thoreau ends this passage with a positive appeal: "But it is a characteristic of wisdom not to do desperate things." Wisdom counteracts the general precursor. One does not have to be hostage to their own negative feelings – because feelings aren't passive. Feelings are activated by the way you think about things – your thoughts. There is good thinking and there is bad thinking, respectively causing good or bad feelings. Wisdom, which Thoreau evokes as a mediator, is sound thinking accessing the highest levels of understanding, truth, relevance, and sensibility. Wisdom allows resolved feelings associated with good mental health.

Precursor 2: Anxiety Triggers

Some time ago, colleges began to provide places on campus for students who are distressed or experiencing anxiety from being exposed to words, ideas, or subjects of discussion. These places are also provided for students who are offended by someone or something. We're not talking about acts of physical hostility or verbal aggression – just words, ideas, and topics. For these people, words, ideas, and topics are triggers for unstable and extreme feelings – anxiety. These designated places on campus prohibit and are free of such triggers. They are called "safe spaces."

Now, college is supposed to be for higher learning. A student attending college will be exposed to ideas, information, and subjects that may be hard for the student to look at intellectually. That's a risk for all students. If the student is enabled to see such exposure as stressful to the point of anxiety that they are justified to have a remedy for it, they will never develop the "ego muscle" necessary to handle the differences and variety in thinking. Ideas, whatever they may be, will never get a chance to inform these people toward refined critical thinking. They will not grow intellectually with mature sensibilities.

I would be embarrassed to need a safe space to escape to and recover from ideas I don't agree with. I want to have an ego muscle developed enough to give me emotional and psychological strength to learn the best of what there is to know and understand. If my ideas are good, challenges to them will reinforce their value. If my ideas are flawed and weak, challenges will cause me to reconsider my ideas and jettison them in favor of new, and hopefully better, ideas.

This "safe space" movement stems in part from things like the Americans with Disabilities Act (ADA) of 1990. The Act mandates that persons with disabilities cannot be discriminated against. Accommodations for disabled persons must be provided so they have access to general public activities. This would include accommodations such as wheelchair ramps for persons using wheelchairs. What grew from that, unfortunately, takes us now to persons who suffer distress and anxiety over words, ideas, and topics. They're seen as disabled and, therefore, need accommodations. Persons who are triggered over words to the extent they suffer serious emotional distress and dysfunction should not be considered disabled in the ADA sense. As kind and helpful as accommodations may seem, they are ultimately harmful to these persons and to society in general as they inhibit a person's intellectual and emotional growth – that person suffers and we all suffer. If a person is truly made anxious by words, ideas, and topics they need a different kind of help than safe spaces can provide.

Precursor 3: Contempt Triggers and Delusion

An intelligent and well-informed patient I counseled many years ago abruptly stated, somewhat agitatedly during a session, that George W. Bush was going to suspend elections and remain in office indefinitely. It was the last part of Bush's second term as president. This was a remarkable thing for the patient to say.

Of course, I was curious where this came from. I already knew the patient disliked Bush to the point of extreme contempt. After I asked several relevant questions, it was easy to determine the patient was delusional, and that his delusion coexisted with an internal contempt trigger causing increased hatred of Bush. This further created a self-fulfilled, false prophecy in the patient. This was a self-feeding psychosis in the patient that would only get stronger without some kind of intervening psychological resolution. I didn't need to use the word "delusional," but I told him by all accounts his prediction was unreasonable.

After Bush left office in the usual way, because his term was completed, the patient insisted that Bush was going to reclaim the presidency – a variation on the patient's original prophecy. Despite reality, of which the patient was well-aware, the delusion was strong and fixed. The core of the delusion was a fixation of unfounded hatred of Bush. To support his hatred of Bush and appear sensible to himself, which is critical, the patient had to have good reason to continue hating Bush, even if he had to make it up. Which he did.

He reasoned Bush was going to retake the presidency. The delusion was a means by which even if the prediction didn't happen he could think, without needing to prove it empirically, Bush fantasized about permanently holding the office of president. The patient would think – *I'm not deluded, Bush is the crazy one, he's narcissistic for thinking he can stay on as president.* Contempt triggered the delusion. A delusion must be fed by a recurring trigger. That's how a delusion operates.

* * *

What can be seen from Precursor 1, Precursor 2, and Precursor 3 is that an affected person is predisposed in some way to some kind of quiet desperation, disordered ideation, and/or delusional thinking. The predisposition is oriented to a resignation of helplessness, anxiety/distress, a fear or expectation of some bad thing to happen, which is internalized pessimistically. For the purpose of discussion, let's identify this foundational predisposition as "Primed for Catastrophe" (PFC).

In the course of living day-to-day, all the things that bother and frustrate you about people comes from the effects of *people who are primed for catastrophe*. Rhetorical nonsense and bad public policy are the result of the abuses of *people with* PFC (PFCs) as well as their being exploited and condescended to by "politically correct (PC) warriors." PFCs are valuable and essential to the political-left (political parties and groups of the left). The political-left assigns and thus burdens PFCs with victim status, tells them the party will champion their cause, gets the PFCs' voices and votes so the political-left can take or stay in power, then abandons them until they are needed again for the next election cycle. An example of this is politicians on the left who demagogue and promise immigration reform to a targeted group of constituent PFCs and sympathetic PFCs, then do nothing in their term in office. (Individuals in racial minorities who refuse to see themselves as victims, even if at times they are, avoid and reject being PFCs. They have escaped the gravitational pull of victimhood and powerless internalized pessimism. They are free, independent, critical thinkers. The political-left has another name for African-Americans in this group; they call them "Uncle Toms.")

In any way that PFCs are validated, or perceive they are violated, their sense of victimhood, worldview, and mental conditions become worse – more victimized, negative, delusional, paranoid, anxious, and hysterical. Imagine the validation for their hysteria PFCs get from the Lee book, discussed previously. PFCs don't even have to read the book, the title alone (*The Dangerous Case of Donald Trump*) will whip them into a frenzy. Moreover, the book fulfills the narrative of the agenda-driven media, which spreads "the word" across the land. These mental afflictions are a contagious virus generated and nourished in PFCs by the agenda-driven media, which behaves as a facilitator and a carrier of the virus. Talk about danger and destruction!

* * *

Trump Derangement Syndrome & Trump Anxiety Disorder

After our discussion on precursors and the role they play in mental instability, we are now ready to discuss derangement and the famous syndrome and disorder associated it. There are two maladjusted psychological conditions created by our *pop/political culture:* "Trump Derangement Syndrome" and "Trump Anxiety Disorder." Let's be clear. We won't find the name Trump in the Axis I section of the *Diagnostic Statistical Manual.* These are not, however, just trendy derogatory references of one political group's swipe across the polarized divide against another political group. These are real clinical conditions; they are mental disorders; and they are epidemic.

Charles Krauthammer, Harvard-educated psychiatrist and pundit, in a December 5, 2003 *Town Hall* article wrote about irrational reactions people had to George W. Bush. In that article, Krauthammer coined the term "Bush Derangement Syndrome" (BDS). He described "the acute onset of paranoia in otherwise normal people in reaction to policies, the presidency – nay – the very existence of George W. Bush." (My patient, previously mentioned, is an example of this.) To be sure, the article was written "tongue-in-cheek," owing to its audience in *pop/political culture*. None the less, the article was serious in identifying a problem; and the description of the phenomenon of BDS was spot on. It fit the clinical standards for diagnostic assessment in accordance with the protocols of the mental status examination.

In today's fierce polarized public discourse with definable cause interests, accusatory claims about the mental instability of public figures who have a voice, a platform, influence, and/or office are rampant. It is, therefore, helpful to clarify the landscape of psychological functioning in terms of politics. Although certainly subject to abuse and misuse, the term BDS has taken on utility beyond rhetorical means by being an accurate identification of a psychological condition from which people suffered on an epidemic scale.

First, take delusion. Any person can be examined for psychological functioning by a competent clinical evaluator to determine if that person is delusional. If delusional, it can be determined if a person has generalized or a specifically focused delusion. If there is delusion, the manifestation of derangement stemming from the delusion can be identified by cognitive/behavior indicators. An example would be a white supremacist activist – with the emphasis on "activist." White supremacist activism is the manifestation of the delusion. (It's also possible to have delusions without their causing psychological distress or dysfunction. For instance, you can believe in unicorns – no problem.)

Second, take derangement. Derangement is when the effects of both distress and dysfunction are manifested. An example of this would be Barbra Streisand's public lament about eating pancakes and putting on excess poundage because Trump's in the White House. (It must be noted, though, it is possible to have intense feelings without having delusion or derangement. That is, you can just dislike or hate someone or something and not be delusional or deranged – you would simply have non-disordered intense feelings.)

Delusion, derangement, and non-disordered intense feelings – all of these psychological variables are readily assessed and determined utilizing mental status examination standards. Irrational, unreasonable, and ridiculous thinking, firmly believed, reveals delusion. Add to this, emotional distress with dysfunction – now you're getting into derangement territory.

Trump Derangement Syndrome

"Trump Derangement Syndrome" (TDS) has not only infected a sizeable percentage of the population, mostly leftists, but it has infected persons across the entire political spectrum. TDS is the same thing as BDS, which Krauthammer identified, with the "trigger cue" being Trump. [We can call the general condition "Whoever/Whatever Derangement Syndrome" (WDS).]

There is a critical distinction to be made here. *Trump is the trigger cue for TDS, not the cause of it. The cause is PFC: Primed for Catastrophe.*

And, the cause *of* PFC is the lack of inherent and/or developed wisdom-mediating thought-processes no matter what feelings are present. Moreover, thought-processes without wisdom and their emersion in widespread media-obsession and hysteria create an almost inescapable echo chamber exponentially fortifying PFC. As noted previously in this chapter, Thoreau told us, "… But it is a characteristic of *wisdom* not to do desperate things." That is, don't act out crazy.

Trump Anxiety Disorder

This brings us to "Trump Anxiety Disorder" (TAD). TAD is basically an offshoot of TDS (reminder: Trump Derangement Syndrome). *Side note:* I don't know about you, but these acronyms get me confused sometimes.

Anyway, anxiety is the persistent dread and worry about something. It can be so intense as to render incapacitation. In the particular case of TAD, you have to start with TDS as the precursor. The complex of TDS/TAD, all the more pernicious due to the irrationality involved, has a harmful cumulative effect on thinking (cognition) – one's judgment and reason. Factors such as association with other likewise-afflicted people, anti-Trump media bias and tirades, protest rallies with hyped media attention, extreme political movements hijacking mainstream political parties, and the pressure not to speak against the political extremist orthodoxy feed and supercharge the effects of TAD. All of such actions are shamefully exploitive and abusive to not only vulnerable people but all people in general.

Hysteria

There's a "sweet spot'" for all things: How much food to eat for enjoyment and nourishment, how much physical exercise to do, how to successfully present a legal argument to a judge or jury, how much taxes should be paid for public services and infrastructure, and so on. In the same way, awareness of danger and threat in your consciousness and psyche has an optimal point for wellness and your ability to function. Hysteria is when concern for danger and threat is moved significantly beyond the sweet spot and becomes irrational fear and obsession.

Hysteria itself is a danger and threat not only to the afflicted hysteric, but to all those in the sphere of contact with that person. And worse, hysteria virally multiplied to mass hysteria is a cancerous scourge on civil society. The many and various protest events – marches and rallies – that have attracted huge numbers of participants feed on hysteria and in turn these events feed hysteria. Organized political movements purposely and effectively exploit this hysteria dynamic. Such movements take advantage of any regularly-present irrational fear that marginally occurs in the general public by fomenting more hysteria until outlooks, decisions, and votes, on a mass scale, are made purely and exclusively on the bases of hysteria.

Speaking of mass hysteria, let's consider the cautionary folk tale of Chicken Little. Variations of the story go back over twenty centuries and across almost all cultures, suggesting the existence of a collective psychological archetype for the concept and message of the tale.

In a widely utilized official folklorist classification system, the Chicken Little story is classified as a cautionary tale of the effects of paranoia and mass hysteria. Some expressions of the story convey the meaning as lighthearted exposure of foolishness. Other interpretations are a grave warning of the danger of widespread hysteria.

The story of Chicken Little evolved from early nineteenth century Europe. The story goes something like this:

This chicken, named Chicken Little, is walking through the woods. On her otherwise lovely walk, an acorn falls from a tree and conks her on her chicken noggin. It startles her, and I bet it hurts. Her immediate and only thought about what's happening is, "The sky is falling!" She says it like that, and loudly, "The sky is falling!"

So, it's not enough this chick gets hit on the head and can likely survive the concussion. She has to think atmospheric air has a physical quality like, I don't know, a massive descending boulder. And then she has to run off in a panic and warn three other fowl feathered friends. And they buy it!

So what else? A fox, wouldn't you know, happens to be nearby and sees an opportunity not to have to worry about his next meal. He approaches the hysterical birds and offers them a fix for their troubles. Now this is interesting, because these birds' natural instinct as prey to correctly react to the real and obvious danger of a predator fox should trump (enjoy the pun) their irrational fear of nothing!

Anyway, the fox escorts these lovely, hysterical, feathered creatures to a place where he puts them out of their misery for good. This also affords him a banquette feast. You might say, "he kills four birds with one appetite."

The cancerous hysteria finding its way into the *pop/political world* is no joke. It is dangerous. The effects of Chicken Little's hysteria is the same as the effects of people's hysteria. They are threatening people and society. We better wake up. Otherwise we'll *lose our grip* and *this Republic, we won't be able to keep.*

And (drum roll) … for your effort and diligence, now that you've read this chapter and you understand it (we'll go by the honor system) you are now a *psychology wonk* on the clinical specialties we covered. *Congratulations!* (cymbal crash)

PART IV

YOU

WHEREVER *YOU* GO, THERE *YOU* ARE. THE ONLY THING *YOU* can't get away from is *you*. The reason *you* are reading this is because of *you*. Living a sensible life is like a high-wire act. It's the art of maintaining the perfect balance between two fundamentally contradictory truths: it's not about *you*, and it's all about *you*.

The remaining chapters of this book invite *you* to look inward. *You* should want to be your best *you*. The essence of conscious living is to make willful decisions about what matters and to live accordingly. As previously discussed, our Republic rests on the virtue and wisdom of our people (see Introduction and Chapter 2). *You* are one of us – our people. Reaching for personal growth and betterment is good for *you* and, through the *butterfly effect*, good for the world.

It's pretty simple – wise people who are good make a good republic.

… it's "*a republic, if you can keep it.*"

CHAPTER 14

In Good We Trust

TOO OFTEN TOO MANY PEOPLE DON'T KNOW THE MEANING of things. Yet they react, many times in a knee-jerk manner, to things they don't understand. A wise and foundational understanding about making decisions in our Republic for our society as a whole is the awareness that those who decide societal laws and policies in our Republic, are fallible. All people are fallible; even good people are fallible. So what can you do? People are all we have to make the decisions that need to be made. So, fallible as we are, even the best of us, what we need to do is reach for a standard.

Good is the standard we need reach for. We don't trust people or a person as much as we trust the standard – *good*. Now, you must have noticed the play on words in this chapter's title. "In God We Trust" became this nation's official motto in 1956. During the Civil War, the public expressed a heightened desire to have a motto remind us of a standard transcendent beyond human fallibility that can be relied upon; the phrase first appeared on U.S. coins in 1864.

This immediately brings us to God … and the idea of God. Well, we've been taking on big ideas in this book, we might as well go for broke and take on the subject of God.

Whether or not you believe in God or some kind of unseen willful higher power, the idea of God is unavoidable in this culture. It's hardwired whether you like it or not. Failing to orient wisely to the best role God plays in people's lives requires dismissal or ignorance of too many relevant, substantial thinkers, past and present.

I don't know if there is a God. And you don't know and nobody else knows either. But I can make a decision. And you and everyone else can make the same kind of decision. That decision is to live as if there is a God.

Throughout my life, I have encountered people all over the spectrum on God, religion, atheism, paganism, agnostic, apathetical, and whatever. Unless you're talking to someone of your persuasion in these matters, debating anyone on God and religion is frustratingly pointless. A person needs to satisfy their intellect, their psychology, and their emotions. So the process of making any sense of this all-important, unwieldy subject is to begin with a non-controversial relatable aspect of human nature: People in general, whether they are good or not, are drawn toward goodness when it's depicted.

Here's the case:

I noticed something about myself and everyone else with regard to movies. In a typical story line with a conflict between good and bad, especially good versus evil, I naturally, with head and heart, root for the good guy; I root for good. Noticing this in everyone I encountered on the subject, even sociopaths, I theorized anecdotally that this was a common way people think and feel. In this regard, movies are highly manipulative as they exploit this general sensibility of people. Movies present an unambiguous portrait of what's good and what's bad, and people's inclination is to root for good. Movie creators intentionally get you to think and feel a particular way; they tap into this universal aspect of human nature to be drawn toward goodness, or what is just and right.

Now let's add another layer of cultural/societal messaging. That would be mainstream religion and religious institutions. In Western culture, for example, despite the infections of corruption, abuses, and atrocities in religious institutions, the generally accepted understanding is religion and religious institutions stand for good, and are good. And, the foundational center of mainstream religions is God.

Whether you reason that God is real or made-up, that at its core God means anything and all things good, you can and should reason that God is another word for good. And, the use of the words "God" and "good" are interchangeable.

Those who say they believe in God very likely, would, without hesitation, say they *do* believe in good. For those who would say they do not believe in God, would they say they *do not* believe in good? I am pleased to verify anecdotally that in discussions over forty years with countless people of all beliefs, people assert they *do* believe in good – that is, they believe in *good* as a value.

So, let's add this up so we can get the meaning. I never have to quarrel with "Is there a God?" When I hear the word "God," whoever said it, however it was meant, I hear the word "good." I have decided to live my life on the basis of being good and doing good. I fail all the time, but I do believe orienting to good is the way to see and understand things.

In lectures I give on the topic, I build the case for this perspective and top it off for impactful reference with this tag line: *God means good. And God is so good He only needs one "O."*

Understanding and Deciding

I have a mythical image of what happens after you die. You get to this heaven-like place and go to a "reconciling station," like a bank teller's window. Only you get to sit down to go over things with the "reconciler." You're going to have to sit because it's going to take some time and may cause shock and disappointment if you find out how wrong you've been about everything. I really like this image. It makes me wonder if people would think and act differently if they believed this is what happens after you die.

There's a scene in Woody Allen's 1977 movie, *Annie Hall*, in which Woody's character, Alvy Singer, is standing in line to see a movie with Diane Keaton's character, Annie Hall. Just in back of them in line is a Columbia University instructor who teaches a class called *TV, Media, and Culture*. He's pontificating to his female companion about the noted contemporary philosopher and intellectual Marshall McLuhan. The guy is expounding on McLuhan's philosophical principles and theses. Overhearing this, Alvy is annoyed by the guy's loud, pompous, and erroneous take on the subject. He finds it insufferable as he complains to Annie Hall. Alvy finally steps out of line, comes forward toward the camera to "break the fourth wall" and addresses us, the audience, with his frustrations. The instructor guy steps out of line to join Alvy, acknowledges us, the audience, and argues his authoritative credentials directly to Alvy. Conveniently, the real Marshall McLuhan is standing off-camera until Alvy brings him into the scene to have him correct the university "expert." McLuhan really puts the instructor in his place, "I heard what you're saying. You know nothing of my work ... How you ever got to teach a course in anything is totally amazing." Alvy then looks into the camera, at us, and says, "Boy, if life were only like this."

Unlike "Professor Know-it-all" in *Annie Hall*, if you understand something well and correctly, and if you are driven by goodness, the decisions you make related to that something will be the best, most sensible, decisions possible. Sensibility is the sum total of available data, variables, compassion, fairness, circumstances, and pragmatism wisely weighed to provide a proper position and decision on any given matter. Everyone has, or should have, a *sensibility meter*. The meter can be thought of as a rating from zero to ten, with zero being no sensibility to ten as the highest level of sensibility.

The reality-TV courtroom genre in which parties contest civil disputes heard and decided by a judge is yet another form of a morality play seated at the table of *pop American culture*. Whenever I watch these dramas, like most people I watch as if I were the judge. I can't think of a time my decision wasn't the same, or nearly the same, as the professional TV judge. Watching like a judge is in essence testing my sensibilities. My good record of agreement with the TV judges' decisions make me feel that in some small way it enhances my sensibility rating toward *ten*.

So, how well do you understand things? And if you think you understand things well, but you really don't, how do you get enlightened? Do you even want to be enlightened? Unfortunately, many people don't understand things as well as they need to, and more unfortunately, they resist enlightenment, if they even know what enlightenment is.

Enlightenment

Whether you desire, resist, or don't know what enlightenment is, let me offer a three-part-perspective you may find helpful:

First, decide by definition that enlightenment is desirable and good. Understand that enlightenment is an on-going process that enhances your life. Enlightenment means you seek to know, understand, and be wise to the end of your conscious days.

Second, know that understanding things on the way towards enlightenment takes some effort. Don't have "knee-jerk" reactions to intellectual stimulus. Wait a beat. Wait two beats or more. You can even wait a day or longer. Slow down and consider things carefully, beginning with the merits of the opposite of what your "knee-jerk" would have been.

Common sense is useful. Common sense is the widespread acceptable way of seeing things – it's conventional wisdom for the masses. But common sense isn't always enough. Not only that, common sense isn't always common. One person's sense of common sense can be different from another person's. So, think hard on what common sense is regarding any given issue.

Then, try to cultivate what I call "uncommon sense." A quick way to understand uncommon sense is to consider the colloquial cliché – "thinking outside of the box." It is sense, but it's not common. There are revelations to be found in uncommon sense; look for them. Uncommon sense is not the usual way to see things. It is not that the usual way is necessarily wrong; the usual way may be very good. This is where wisdom comes in – "unconventional wisdom" – wisdom with depth, not often seen in the masses. Such "unconventional wisdom" is the mediator of the continuum from common sense to uncommon sense.

Common sense, uncommon sense, and wisdom make up "the trilogy of understanding" – your pathway to enlightenment. And enlightenment is *good.*

Third, develop a "team" of thinkers drawn from the "pages" of history who are representative of your *thought ethos*. A *thought ethos* is your willful psychological/intellectual/values profile. It encompasses your world view. To be a relevant person, a consequential person, and have a chance for personal fulfillment you need to have a *thought ethos*; but you shouldn't just slap one together like a Mr. Potato Head toy. You need to take some time to research and think it through so the "team" of thinkers representing your *thought ethos* reflects the best of who you are and how you think.

The thinkers on your "profile team" should include philosophers, theologians, scientists, politicians, warriors, and artists from various cultures and geographies. There should be at least two representatives from each of the following periods in history: ancient times, the Middle Ages, the Renaissance, the Enlightenment, the Industrial Revolution, fifty years ago, and two who are alive today. These thinkers should illustrate "the trilogy of understanding."

On top of this, you should have a mentor in your life – a living person to keep you in line who also possesses "the trilogy."

Doing all of this is no guarantee you'll approach, obtain, and maintain enlightenment. But if you pick the right thinkers and the right mentor, and you value goodness as a standard, you'll have your best shot at the golden ring of enlightenment. "The golden ring of enlightenment" – reminds me of Bill Murray's character, Carl Spackler, in the movie *Caddyshack* who recounts his encounter with the Dalai Lama as His Holiness's caddy. (I know, the image is funny.) Spackler recounts that after the round of golf, he didn't receive a money tip from His Holiness. Instead for his tip, the Dalai Lama told Spackler that he will receive *total consciousness* (something like enlightenment) on his death bed. Spackler remarks reflectively about his tip from the Dalai Lama, "So I got that going for me." In your case, it would be nice not to have wait until you die to have enlightenment. You *can* live an ever-growing enlightened life beginning now.

So, go forth and be wise ... and enlightened.

CHAPTER 15

Intelligence or Stupidity?

NEVER UNDERESTIMATE A PERSON'S INTELLIGENCE OR their stupidity. All of us have both intelligence and stupidity. This includes the best of us and the worst of us, as well as societies' leaders. I certainly know this of myself, as well. The interplay of intelligence and stupidity has a continuous impact on cultural, societal, political, and governmental functioning.

In the course of running public affairs, decisions on all matters across a spectrum from irrelevant to critical invariably encounter controversy. Imagine that controversies are discussed and intellectually processed with the idea of presenting compelling arguments to persuade toward a decision based on what is relevant to the matter. Further imagine if a strong position is held on a matter there would still be earnest curiosity to hear another position that could be persuasive based on the merits … as John Lennon said, "Imagine."

This kind of discourse rarely plays out in the vast media forum. In most media platforms, the discourse of controversies plays out like an extreme caricature of the proverbial professional wrestling match with promotional build-up hype. (Which is an insult to professional wrestling.) Media coverage of politics exists to create the "body-slam/gotcha" move. Media must have its villain and hero, its Christ and antichrist. The actual controversies, the focus on decisions for public policy, the things that really matter are ignored and put aside by the media. In the worst way, what is presented by the media are Neanderthal goons on different teams going at each other to fight over, not discuss, the most consequential issues of the day.

To the people who know me or know something about me, I have a little bit of "street cred." If I find myself in a discussion in which I'm willing to engage, I may say something unexpected and/or provocative. Usually, because of my *bona fides* and "street cred" people will pause to hear more about what I mean. Likewise, I'm also interested in what they have to say. It's gratifying.

Unfortunately, in the public arena such mature thoughtful discourse is not the norm. And worse, the distorted, cartoon caricature that does play out in public discourse passes as true and is accepted unquestioned.

* * *

Our Republic is susceptible to what I call "political dark ages." These are times when polarizations of special interests, values, and politics create a stagnation, preventing constructive progress, across-the-board, for individuals and society as a whole. It took the American Civil War to end the dark age of slavery and the rot it caused society. It didn't take long to enter the next political dark age, which was ignited by the assassination of President Lincoln. We are currently living in a political dark age that may have started when the stock market crashed in October 1929, leading to the Great Depression. This present dark age was temporarily interrupted during World

War II. It resumed during the Cold War, and continues. Because of the progression of widespread improvement in the standard of living unsurpassed in history; societal affluence; collective attention deficit; the 24-hour news cycle; and the small-minded, childish, pathological need to have a boogieman, we have arrived at a new chapter of this dark age – the "age of Trump."

The Age of Trump

During this continuing dark age, those who have held leftist views know little or nothing about people who are conservative. Leftists generally have serious misconceptions about conservatives, such as their being anti-LBGT...etc., or anti-environment, or anti-other-than-white, or anti-women, or anti-compassion, or anti-decent. For the left, the purpose of these misconceptions is to be a basis for dehumanizing and/or vilifying conservatives, relieving leftist from engaging in thoughtful, respectful discussion of issues. Leftists can simply dismiss conservatives, or anyone who doesn't tow the leftist orthodoxy, as unworthy, soulless creatures. This poisonous lie continues to fuel the present dark age. Our political discourse has been purposefully held hostage by an intentional fallacy: the untruth of conservative/Republican bigotry. On the other hand, partly due to the tyranny of political correctness, conservatives generally know and understand leftists very well; they understand leftist positions and can be sympathetic to concerns and causes that leftists have. Leftists generally either don't know or won't accept this.

Signs

There are, however, in the "age of Trump," signs we can, and may, break free of this self-inflicted stupidity and emerge from the darkness into the light of a new and healthy day. This will be our turning point to "the better angels of our nature" as Abraham Lincoln put it.

A remarkable event took place in the Oval Office of the West Wing at the White House. It received much press attention, mostly from the anti-Trump media, which completely misreported what happened in terms of its true significance, revealing the underlying panic the anti-Trump media feel from the sense they are losing their propaganda onslaught, nay, campaign:

Kanye West was paying a visit to his new pal President Trump. (There are some people you just sit back and let them do their "thing" – Kanye is one of those people.) There, in the Oval office, so crowded with reporters and their camera crews it was a fire marshal's nightmare, with President Trump sitting at the Commander in Chief's desk – he sat back silently (odd for Trump) and drank up what Kanye was pouring. In his rambling but wise words Kanye exclaimed, "You think racism can control me? Oh that don't stop me. That's an invisible wall."

The left didn't like this. We have a high profile, African-American man, wearing a M-A-G-A cap, speaking his own signature vernacular, who has a huge fan base, showing his alignment and affinity with Trump (everything the left is against). Events like this show the left is losing ... but we're not out of these darks ages yet.

I can tell you the bellwether that will signify the end of this dark age: To the extent that racism, sexism, hostility to sexual-orientation/gender-identity ranges, and xenophobia exists, this political dark age will end when these rampant negative views and bigotries are attributed to anyone who actually holds these sick views and are not definitionally attributed to conservatives and Republicans as a group; when victim-status ceases to carry any political capital – when that day comes – this dark age will be behind us, and Martin Luther King's dream will be realized!

* * *

Trump Haters

For those of you who despise Trump to the core in ways you never before had such contempt for a world figure you don't personally know, you are at risk for letting your Trump-hate miss a one-time opportunity to realize the things you care about to come to fruition. You don't have to like Trump. You can continue to hate him to your heart's content, but don't be stupid by squandering a chance to have the things you care about happen in your lifetime.

Get this, I'll put it simple to you: *Trump is a market correction!* Before he was elected our collective political practices were causing any efforts at good governance to crash and burn. And, if you didn't know that you should've. Our system was fine. Our governance politicians were horrible to the extreme.

There were about 8.4 million voters who voted for Barack Obama who also voted for Donald Trump. Some kind of change was wanted … and needed. It wasn't the system that needed change, it was the swamp. The 2016 election was a referendum against political dynasties, political corruption, and political nonsense. *Trump is a market correction.*

Trump's a disrupter. Whatever your politics and philosophy, you were never going to get your way until there was a shake-up to get the *stupid* out. With Trump we, you, can get the reset needed. He's already doing it. *He is a market correction.*

You don't have to be stupid and worry about Trump. There are no reports that Trump raped anybody, like the reports about Bill Clinton. Past claims of Trump's sexual scuminess on things that have public significance have not been substantiated. If they are substantiated we can deal with it appropriately. Trump hasn't rounded-up people for internment camps, like Franklin Roosevelt did. Trump hasn't committed genocide, like Joseph Stalin, Adolf Hitler, and Pol Pot. Trump hasn't imprisoned, journalist like Lincoln did during the Civil War. Trump hasn't used his power as president nor did he support the enactment of legislation to stop the media or press hostile to him, like John Adams did in his presidency.

Instead, Trump put more money in your pocket, whether you like him or not. Trump actively orchestrated the return of political hostages and prisoners from totalitarian regimes without payment or concessions, whether you like him or not. Trump initiated a process to neutralize the nuclear threat from the most rogue and repressive regime on the planet, whether you like him or not. Trump enacted service responsiveness and administrative accountability in the heretofore failing Department of Veteran Affairs, whether you like him or not. Trump signed a water infrastructure act to improve the nation's rivers, harbors, and drinking water; among the many provisions targeted in this act is an overhaul to the system of providing for clean water so the atrocity of what happened in Flint Michigan is not repeated, whether you like him or not.

Bill Maher said a remarkable thing on his HBO show *Real Time*, "… this economy is going pretty well … I feel like the bottom has to fall out … and by the way, I'm hoping for it because I think one way you get rid of Trump is a crashing economy. So please, bring on the recession. Sorry if it hurts people." Maher would rather *you* go through financial hardship, which means for many lost jobs, homes, marriages, children, possible suicide, and worse, than have Trump in office, because Maher, who's wealthy and won't suffer at all in a bad economy, doesn't like Trump. Look, it comes down to you have to like/love your country more than you hate Trump, or anyone else for that matter.

More than anything, half the population needs to grow-up. Everything is not going to be perfect, so grow-up and stop crying about every stupid thing you don't like, whether it's bathrooms or showing ID to vote. Stop being concrete and stupid.

Even if you didn't vote for Trump and you hate his guts, you're lucky because he cleared the board for you. Now, you have a chance you didn't have before.

Election for president comes every four years. Four years is a good time span for a presidential term. It's enough time for a president to show leadership and political effectiveness. But four years is not too long if you're dissatisfied. If you have a better choice than Trump vote for that person. But here's a piece of advice from the "trilogy of understanding" (see Chapter 14), the person you vote for should run on ideas, not Trump-hatred.

The majority of the stupid is invincible and guaranteed for all time. The terror of their tyranny, however, is alleviated by their lack of consistency. —Albert Einstein

I agree with Albert's first sentence. I'm much less certain about his second sentence. Vigilance toward goodness and wisdom is the key to a *stronger, firmer grip* on "*if you can keep it.*"

CHAPTER 16

Voter Guide

WAY TOO MANY ELECTED OFFICIALS ARE IDIOTS. THEY'RE clueless, lacking vision and relevance. On top of that is the corruption they wreak. It's truly a wonder how they get elected and reelected. It's not necessarily because voters are idiots too, although it's a factor. For the most part, many voters are just asleep at the wheel, if they're at the wheel at all. It's likely this is precisely why Franklin said, "… *if you can keep it.*"

So, Let's Do a Better Job at Voting

Your vote isn't the only way to influence electoral outcomes. You can give money, raise money, volunteer for candidates and causes, be on action committees, be in the media or press, tell a friend, commit voter fraud, and more. To be clear I'm not recommending voter fraud. Actually, I would like to take this opportunity to warn you against committing voter fraud, or doing anything fraudulent for that matter.

Even though there are legitimate ways to exponentially expand your influence in an election, most everybody who bothers to vote

147

does so with a single ballot. Keep this in mind though: Depending on where you live, if you take into account a variety of expenses and the multitude of hourly costs to get your vote, if you take all the candidates and cause-initiatives on a ballot, the combined campaign organizations for those candidates and cause initiatives you voted for, just your votes on your ballot could come to a cost of as much as $20,000. Too bad for you they didn't pay you directly. Your single vote is valuable; you shouldn't waste it like so many people do.

Public service ads hyping people to get out and vote generically, as if it doesn't matter how you vote because voting is just so good, are ridiculous and irresponsible. There are, however, strategic campaigns that look generic but are playing to a target market of a predetermined left-leaning base, usually younger people who are lazy about voting. *Rock the Vote* is one such politically progressive organization. The message is it's not only your civic duty, it's cool to vote. So, just vote! This encourages too many people to vote who don't know anything about the issues or anything. I want those people to stay out of it. I only want high-volume voting for my picks.

On that note, I'm in favor of having to register every voting cycle. To be eligible to vote in a particular cycle you would need to be a citizen and demonstrate understanding of the issues by passing a test. (Now that's how voter suppression should be done.) I'm not holding my breath this will ever happen. For the most part I have a positive disposition, but I'm making a point that our current system relies on an electorate that doesn't know enough. I don't want to be paranoid, but I see you people, and you got me worried. I'm worried about a tipping point of just one vote in the wrong direction. We can lose it all! Remember – it's *a loose grip*.

If asked, I don't mind telling people how to vote. But I don't tell them without first saying what I care about. With voting, you start with your values. That's the point of my vote. I don't vote for a candidate based on whether I like them personally. It's nice if you do like them: but I vote issues, not likeability. Yep, it's all about values.

Have a Basic Set of Values, here's mine:

I care to live as free as possible to do what I want. I want to keep as much of the money I work for as possible for myself to do with it what I want. Because I don't trust totalitarian regimes, I want America to have the most sophisticated, efficient, best-trained, best-equipped military peace force in the world.

I know business doesn't care about me other than the money I spend to buy their products and services. Still, business, the free market, provides the highest quality of life for the lowest cost to the greatest number of people, as has been demonstrated throughout the world with America leading the way. Other than sufficiently providing for veterans via the Veterans Administration (which continues to need a major overhaul), I want the federal government to stay out of medical delivery and patient care to the general public. I want the federal government out of education. The free market won't pass up an opportunity to use the profit-incentive model of private industry to effectively provide for the needy, coordinated through community service leagues the same way America had a robust network of mutual aid societies in the nineteenth and early twentieth centuries. Food, housing, clothing, medical care, education, jobs, child care, and more would be provided much better to those in need if government stepped away.

Now for the Vote

President Barack Obama essentially shut down considerations, discussions, and negotiations with congressional Republicans over tax reductions for small businesses, prophetically telling House Majority Leader Eric Cantor, "Elections have consequences." They sure do, Mr. President, for better or worse, they sure do.

Voting is a strategic act to bring about good governance. It's not for sending a message. Voting your conscience often doesn't fit with voting for someone who has a chance to win and advance the things you care about. Unless reliable polls show otherwise in a campaign cycle, voting for a third party candidate is throwing your $20,000 vote away.

Donald Trump is a third party candidate. Apparently he was serious about being president as he rightly took his third party, the "Trump Party" with its sensibilities, to run as a Republican. Bernie Sanders did exactly the same thing by taking the "Bernie Party" to run as a Democrat. He might very well have gotten the Democratic nomination if Hillary hadn't had magical "superdelegate votes" of which party leaders corruptly approved.

Your vote is binary. It's this guy or that guy, or gal, as the case may be. Your vote doesn't know anything about nuance, ambivalence, or your heart. It's like your laptop, tablet, and smart phone; they all operate on a binary system. That's what makes voting and your cell phone apps work. *Side note:* Voting and apps will probably come together some day, if they haven't already.

It's not always clear what polls tell, but pay attention to them and try to understand as best you can what's going on. From there, get out of your own way. Whether or not you like the candidate personally, whether or not for some reason a candidate rubs you the wrong way, keep your eye on the prize and vote for the person who's more likely to align with things you care about. It's that easy. *Elections do have consequences:* it's "*a republic, if you can keep it.*"

CHAPTER 17

So, If You Want To Keep It

IF YOU WANT TO KEEP OUR REPUBLIC WITH THE VALUES AND principles established by the founders this is what enough of us need to do:

1) Know and understand the history of Western civilization and this nation.
2) Continue to learn without limits.
3) Know what's good and value it.
4) Cultivate wisdom and maintain it.
5) Be sensible, especially when it's necessary.
6) Be kind and generous.
7) Have a good sense of humor.

The chapters in this book encompass these seven things. Do these things and *a loose grip* gets *stronger and firmer …* and *we will keep it – our great Republic!*

CHAPTER 18

To Be Continued...

WHILE WORKING ON *A LOOSE GRIP*, I HAVE BEEN SPEAKING at events discussing today's *pop/political culture* and the rampant political psychosis across our society. I have been talking about the principles, observations, and conclusions laid out in this book. *A Loose Grip* wasn't yet completed and my audiences wanted to know when a sequel was going to be available. Now, that's a population hungry for the answers to the challenges of our society, for now and the future.

This page is being written the day Robert Mueller reported that his investigation was complete, and there would be no indictments of Trump, or anyone from his campaign, for colluding with Russia during the 2016 presidential election – the "stated" reason the two-year investigation was launched in the first place. Indeed, as Sonny and Cher sang, "The beat goes on ..."

Since I began *A Loose Grip*, new political figures have come on the scene. There are full-scale battles over immigration policies that are choking-off reason and functionality. There are congressional investigations being weaponized against political differences. There are loud voices calling for a socialist wave to cleanse the ills of capitalism; and it seems those same loud voices have had it with fossil fuels and cow farts. There are new regulations in some states allowing babies who are born to be made "comfortable" while the mother and her doctor decide whether the baby lives or is put to death.

And, there is a presidential election fast approaching that will be a referendum on the "Trump" *Market Correction.*

The beat goes on …

Ergo, if the "book gods" will it so, there will be a sequel to *A Loose Grip* … I wonder what the title will be?

Stay tuned …

Afterword

WANT TO TELL YOU WHAT I THINK AND HOW I FEEL AFTER having written this book, *A Loose Grip*. Despite the subjects specifically tied to the current topical concerns discussed in this book, I have in some way been writing this book my entire consciously reflective life.

I think it was the right time for me to I write this book. Like a race horse at the starting gate, it was on hold in my mind, waiting to burst out when I sat down at my laptop and said in my head, "It's *a loose grip*." I pretty much knew everything I was going to write and how it would be organized. Despite knowing my subjects well, I obsessively researched everything for multiple checks, and learned new things along the way. I wrote it at a very fast pace. But I often got stalled with passages that needed to be better written. Many times I would stare at the screen and go back and forth, inserting and deleting the same word. It didn't frustrate me; I actually enjoyed doing that.

This book is not a passion project, although it is heavily ego invested. *I want it to be read!* I have a strong sense that it needs to be read. It's not that I say things in the book that people are thinking but haven't said. Plenty of smart people are thinking and saying these things. It's not original enlightenment. It is, however, like a musician, my original stylings that I know many people can relate to and find intellectual alignment with. I've seen it already.

You have responsibilities as an individual and we have responsibilities as a society. This book, my voice, is joining other voices to assert the value of unalienable rights and to use this Republic as a vehicle for those rights.

I was asked once by someone who was trapped in his fashion-tribe of cynicism why I cared about this stuff so much. I told him, "I can't help but care." I have a high sensory alert for cognitive dissonance in others, and particularly in myself. Politics and worldview are a minefield of cognitive dissonance. It causes "noise" in my head and a rush of intellectual activity to make sense of the minefield. I go into hyper-mode, eliminate concrete thinking, and turn on raw critical analysis. It's what I have done in writing *A Loose Grip*.

By the way, the guy who asked me why I cared, as if it was a waste of time and energy, wound-up admitting to me how much this stuff does affect him; he thinks about it all the time. How is that for cognitive dissonance *and* projective identification?

That's my point, this, the stuff I've written about in this book, affects all of us. I just want to unpack it publically, via this book, as a service to you and our Republic.

Please share this book with others. It can make a positive impression.

Glossary

Check it out. It's fun and informative.

WORDS HAVE MEANING. SO DO TERMS AND PHRASES. Particularly in context. I like to have a guide to make sure my comprehension is good. You probably know the words in this glossary, but if you're not sure, this should help. In some cases, I'm giving dictionary definitions. In other cases, I'm providing my definitional interpretation relevant to contextual understanding. The term "in context" refers to how a word, term, or phrase is used in this book – *A Loose Grip*.

Introduction

"Experiment" – This refers to the idea that America as a civilization; a nation; and a government of the people, by the people, and for the people is not a certainty as to its success and durability. The term "experiment" is a humble reminder of how great nations of the past have fallen. The experiment is whether the founders came up with the right formula for governance. Stay tuned.

Object Relations Theory – This refers to how a person relates to the people and things in their life. It is a developmental theory,

159

as it identifies the first relationship that a new born has is with a mother or mother figure. How well or not-well the relationship is will have implications for adjustment and well-being throughout life. In context, object relations defines your worldview.

Catharsis – Is a breakthrough of meaningful emotional release and intellectual connection to that emotion. It is a positive psychological process, enhancing growth and resolution.

Feudalism – A system of agreements and exchanges based on a land economy. The feudal system flourished in Europe, in one form or another, between the ninth and fifteenth centuries. A complex hierarchical network of kings, lords, and peasants maintained a mutual bond in exchange for land, military protection, labor, housing, food, and loyalty. The feudal system had elements of totalitarianism, socialism, communism, slavery, capitalism, corruption, betrayal, rule of law, and cooperation. Regional disputes were common, as were military hostilities or the threat thereof.

Part I

Exceptionalism – Being exceptional and unique. Like no other. With the suffix "ism," this usually refers to a nation. In context, exceptionalism refers to the United States of America. It is meant as a positive, noteworthy attribute of this nation. In recent times, as a result of attitudes in political correctness, there has been controversy about the term as it relates to America.

Jingoistic – Behavior showing a strong, unreasonable belief in the superiority of your own country; extreme chauvinism; belligerent foreign policy.

Political Correctness – Avoidance of all forms of expression, particularly language and speech, perceived to exclude, marginalize, or insult groups of people. The level of sensitivity and "correctness" required by those who care, or want to look like they care, can be extreme and absurd. In context, political correctness chokes off and debilitates any serious and thoughtful discussion of important subjects. Political correctness hijacks all meaning and relevance, and gives over to nonsense and small mindedness. Political correctness can be a straw-man in itself. It is often disreputably used in identity politics.

"The Experiment" – See Introduction in Glossary.

Industrial Revolution – A period from about the late eighteenth century to about the mid-nineteenth century. The period ushered in a groundswell of technical advances in machinery and mass production in manufacturing. It began in Britain and spread worldwide.

Alien and Sedition Acts – Among many things these Acts imposed restrictions on speech or other expressions opposing the Adams administration of the federal government – not very First Amendment*y*. These Acts were a response to concerns about impending war with France during the period of about 1790 to the beginning of the 1800s. War was averted. These Acts, which were signed into law by John Adams, likely cost him reelection. Ironically, the Alien and Sedition Acts were also against the principles Adams had fought hard to establish, of which he was well aware. To be fair, I don't think Adams meant any harm. I have done much research on Adams throughout my life. Despite a sometimes obnoxious personality, he is one of my heroes. He's one of three people I believe that without, there would not be a United States of America. The other two are Benjamin Franklin and George Washington.

Chapter 1

Sovereign Human Society (Sovereign Nation) – Freedom from external control: Autonomy, especially: an autonomous state.

Stylings – The particular stylized ways that distinguish a person from other people. A person's talents, personality, quirks, temperaments, creativities, ingenuities, strengths, and weaknesses.

Vito Corleone – This is a pop-culture reference to the patriarchal head of the crime family from the novel and movie *The Godfather*. The main character, Vito Corleone, famously said, "I'm going to make him an offer he can't refuse." Trust me, you don't want that kind of offer. Used in this context, I'm just having some fun.

Fire Sale – A sale of goods at extremely discounted prices. The term originated in reference to damaged goods, such as from a fire. But the meaning has expanded to selling off inventory at low prices to get urgently needed revenue. In context, this is a metaphor describing the international circumstances during the Jefferson presidency. In addition to other intrigues, France needed money quickly to help fund wars in Europe.

Treaty-Lingo-Kabuki – I devised this off-the-cuff term to refer to something like "the art of the deal," the pop/classic book title Donald Trump is known for. It's a mixed metaphor, combining the language (lingo) and intricacies of international treaties and the concept of Japanese kabuki theater as showy, manipulative, and not always to be trusted. In regard to the Louisiana Purchase, this is a slightly cynical reference to what it takes to close a deal. The cynicism is probably disrespectful and not completely justified on my part. The Louisiana Purchase was a great deal for America.

Is – It means is.

Chapter 2

The Enlightenment – A European intellectual, philosophical, and scientific movement that took place from about the seventeenth to the eighteenth century. The tenets of reason and individuality were explored, hypothesized, discussed, and written about during this time.

Unalienable Rights – As a human being, these are rights that cannot be given up even if the holder of that right, which is anybody, wants to. They're rights that exist by the nature of being a person.

Factoid – A trivial fact. It may or may not be true, but it is acknowledged for having some notable acceptance. The writer Norman Mailer coined the term in his book about Marilyn Monroe. The suffix, "oid" means appearance or form.

E Pluribus Unum – Latin for – from many one. Or, out of many one. It was a motto that appeared on the Great Seal of the United States at the time of the seal's creation. It refers to the union formed by the states. But the meaning has stretched to the idea that many people from diverse origins, ethnicities, and nationalities come together to be one people, Americans.

Chapter 3

Mensa – An international organization in which membership is based on superior intelligence quotient (IQ). Boy, I want to be smarter all the time. The measurement of intelligence is not without controversy. But expert consensus on current assessments include general knowledge as a component of intelligence, or IQ. In this way, IQ is not fixed. You can increase your IQ by increasing your knowledge. That's how I try to get smarter. Organizing your thinking along logical disciplines also exercises your intelligence muscle. So, hopefully, writing this book made *me* smarter. And hopefully, reading this book makes *you* smarter. Wisdom, that's another thing all together. I wonder if there is an organization for people with superior wisdom. It might be useful to have a reliable wisdom quotient (WQ).

Mona Lisa – One of the most iconic works of art, known throughout the world. Leonardo da Vinci painted this portrait of a woman who is thought to be the wife of a cloth merchant. Leonardo captured an emotional subtlety that is considered artistically innovative for the time. The painting is thought to be a sublime piece of work, and currently hangs in the Louvre Museum in Paris, France.

Indulgences – This started to take shape in the eleventh century. It was a concoction of the Roman Catholic Church to generate revenue by selling indulgences to the church faithful. What did you get for your money? Less punishment in the afterlife. Over time, this "service/commodity" got wildly out of hand. The priest and theologian Martin Luther saw through this "snake oil" corruption and protested it. The Protestant Reformation comes from the word "protest."

Magna Carta – This was a revolutionary document the monarch of England, King John, was forced to sign in 1215. It was a notable historical signal that divine dictatorial rule of absolute authority was inevitably unsustainable. A monarch, no matter how powerful, is accountable to more than just himself. Despite poor, inconsistent, and at times nonexistent enforcement of the *Magna Carta*, it has had a strong effect throughout the world. Although its origins and purpose were to serve the landowning noble class, it eventually became the rough foundation for the rights of all people no matter their class.

Feudalism – See Introduction in Glossary.

Direct Relationship Doctrine – Prior to the Reformation, religious conviction and salvation were a "brokered" arrangement between the observant and the priests of the Roman Catholic Church. The invention of the printing press brought about more access to literature and holy scripture, as well as increased literacy in general. This contributed to the Reformation movement and was both a demonstration and vehicle for direct connection and relationship with God and Christ without the requirement of a priest.

The Reformation – A movement in the sixteenth century against abuses and corruption in the Roman Catholic Church. This resulted in the establishment of many denominations of Reformed and Protestant Churches.

The Enlightenment – See Chapter 2 in Glossary.

Common Sense – A pamphlet written by Thomas Paine and published in 1776. It challenged the authority of British government and laid out arguments for American independence. It was widely-read and popular. Its influence demonstrated how *the pen can be mightier than the sword.* In this case, "the pen" helped lead to "the sword."

"The Experiment" – See Introduction in Glossary.

Vassal – Under the feudal system (see Feudalism in Introduction in Glossary), a vassal was subservient and loyal to the feudal lord in exchange for protection. It's a harsh life without freedom, a kind of slavery.

Grievance Class – I devised this term to refer to groups, coalitions, organized activists, and individuals who make and align with grievances and complaints as the sole purpose of their (the grievance class) existence. Many grievances may have reasonable merit, but too often they not only lack merit, they are foolish.

Moreover, there is an emotional component to the complaint in which the merits are less important than the act of complaining itself – for the grievance class, making grievances and complaints is a compulsion.

Chapter 4

Totalitarian – Of or relating to centralized control by an autocratic leader or hierarchy, authoritarian, dictatorial, especially despotic, of or relating to a political regime based on subordination of the individual to the state and strict control of all aspects of the life and productive capacity of the nation, especially by coercive measures (such as censorship and terror).

Ad hominem – Appealing to feelings or prejudice rather than intellect. Attacks on an opponent's character rather than answering the contentions made.

Straw-man – Purposely and disingenuously misrepresenting an argument. It deflects from what is true and relevant. Fake argument.

Atrocity – I dislike the inaccurate use of the word "tragedy" when atrocity is the correct word. These words have different meanings. It's a tragedy when a flood wipes out your home. It's an atrocity when a gunmen wipes out people at a café.

Dark Divides – I devised this term to refer to political/social divides that are rooted in hatred, ignorance, cruelty, and destruction.

Toxic Divide of Destruction – I devised this term as an expansion on the previous term to refer to the ill-effects of "dark divides" in relation to their toxicity and destructiveness.

Pop/Political – I devised this term to refer to the merger of popular interest and politics with implications of fashion, tribalism, activism, and adherence to other such groups of like minds.

Pop/Political Culture – I devised this term as an expansion of the previously identified term "pop/political." In context, referring to the cultural state and impact.

Chapter 5

Abridging – In context, deprive, depriving.

Sovereign Nation – See Chapter 1 in Glossary.

Exceptionalism – See Part I in Glossary.

Lady Justice – A symbolic personification of the legal system. Portrayed in America as a blindfolded woman, dressed in a classical toga, carrying a sword and set of scales representing fair and equal administration of the law, without corruption, greed, prejudice, or favor.

Unalienable Rights – See Chapter 2 in Glossary.

The Alien and Sedition Acts – See Part I in Glossary.

Alas – It's an old fashion word. It's an exclamation of grief, pity, or concern. My editor penciled it in and I liked it. It was a good addition to the text and I thought it gave a Shakespearian flare. We should use old words that have style and meaning to keep them alive. "Alas, I wish we all spoke better."

Politically Correct – See political correctness in Part I in Glossary.

Fake News – The term Donald Trump branded to convey the disreputable, propagandistic, contemptuous reporting, and punditry by the press. The term has wide popular appeal to people who align with Trump's view of a large segment of the press; and conversely, the term draws disdain from large anti-Trump factions.

Gestapo – The state secret police for Nazi Germany during the Third Reich. They were political police who ruthlessly eliminated opposition or perceived opposition to the Nazis, often using thuggish and murderous means. In context, the reference to Gestapo-like is to describe metaphorically the organized ruthlessly violent tactics of extreme political activist groups for the purpose of intimidation and terror on college campuses and elsewhere.

"The Mob" – In context, this refers to organized extreme political activist groups who use physical violence against people as well as committing property destruction. Mainstream news organizations sympathetic to the mob's politics, but not openly approving the violence, often object to the term "mob." The term is intended to be an accurate descriptive pejorative and reflects the political polarizations and contempt associated with the hyper-political climate.

De Facto – It means *in fact* in Latin. However, the use of this term conveys additional meaning – in effect, as something that can be seen as factual by default because of common acceptance and understanding without official identification as factual.

Book Burning – A form of censorship and intellectual restriction by a regime. Books are burned in public as a display and warning to people about thoughts and ideas that are unacceptable in the regime, and may be subject to criminal penalty. In a free society, there may be hate speech, but would you rather have hate speech or mind-control book burnings?

Chapter 6

Ethos – The distinguishing character, sentiment, moral nature, and guiding beliefs of a person, group, or institution.

Fake – You know the word "fake." It means phony. The reason it appears in this glossary is to highlight the specific pop/political cultural meaning the word acquired during the Trump era.

Donald Trump created the brand "fake," which could arguably be the reason, in combination with other branded words and phrases, he was elected to the presidency. I purposely used the word "fake" in various parts of this book to remind us of its influence and its pop/political context.

Fashion Tribe – I devised this term to refer to the forces of "fashion science/sociology/ideology" that forms groups, allegiances, and orthodoxy centered around strong group affiliations. This can be oriented around politics, religion, philosophy, sports, family, professions, and more.

Fashion Warrior – I devised this term to refer to the metaphorical warfare on the grounds of fashion identification in regard to political tribalism.

Non Sequitur – It means *does not follow* in Latin. An intellectual argument that lacks a string of logic. A preceding point does not fit with a following point. So, don't think or speak in *non sequiturs* – you won't make sense.

Rorschachian – This is a play on the meaning of the projective inkblot test devised by Hermann Rorschach. The way I use this term in context is a reference to the psychological process of seeing what you want to see in a person, an event, or an idea. Some things or people are susceptible to being projected onto by another source (a person, a media format, or other) . Many factors can create such projection susceptibility.

Cognitive Dissonance – Is having a conflict of feelings, beliefs, and ideas with your own or others' behavior and reality. Cognition is the way you think. Dissonance is anything that goes against the way you think or is disruptive to an idea. In political matters, cognitive dissonance is regularly present, particularly if your politics aren't credible or sound. If you're not emotionally uncomfortable when this happens, it suggests some psychopathology. If you are emotionally uncomfortable you can resolve the dissonance and emotional discomfort with rationalization, which is a collapse of intellectual integrity. Or you can change your thinking to align with reality, indicative of strong character and intellectual integrity.

Part II

No terms from this section.

Chapter 7

Tectonic Shifts – Tectonic Shifts are a geological phenomenon. It refers to the roughly dozen major plates and several minor plates of the Earth's crust that are in constant motion. In context, the reference is something having a strong and widespread impact. As a metaphor in politics, the shift is a major change with profound consequences.

Litmus Test – In chemistry, it's a test for a solution's property of acidity to alkalinity. In colloquial meaning, it refers to a decisive indicator based on a related index of something. In context, it's an unreasonable, unwarranted, and incorrect assumption about someone based on a political position or a politician one supports.

Reactionary – This word is usually associated with right-wing extremist views towards progressivism or left-wing philosophy. In context, this term is used to refer to extreme reactive negative attitude and behavior toward Trump as well as those who support Trump or those who are just neutral about Trump.

Electoral College – The presidential ticket is elected by a selected group of 538 electors of the Electoral College. The ticket has to receive at least 270 votes from the electors to win the presidency. Each state gets an allotment of electors. The electors can vote as they choose, but they most always vote according to the popular vote from their state. The distribution of electors is structured so regions with greater populations don't have an advantage over regions of smaller populations.

Amorphous – Having no definite form, being without definite character or nature: Unclassifiable.

Fake – See Chapter 6 in Glossary.

Brexit States – In context, the term borrows the word "Brexit" from the political movement of Britain exiting the European Union. Britain (Br) and "exit" from the word "Brexit." The term "Brexit states" is a play on the word "Brexit" and refers to the Midwest states with a regional economy affecting a political break from previous voting patterns.

Repoed – Past tense of *repo*, short for "repossessed." This short term has come to be the standard term used to refer to a repossession of a car or any item when a buyer defaults on payments.

Ad hominem – See Chapter 4 in Glossary.

Cathartically – Adverb of catharsis. See Introduction in Glossary.

Cognitive Dissonance – See Chapter 6 in Glossary.

Double Cognitive Dissonance – See Chapter 6 in Glossary. In context, I added the "double" to refer to the compounding of the cognitive dissonance process.

Chapter 8

Fake – See Chapter 6 in Glossary.

Forensics – As this relates to psychology, the focus is on clinical assessment. A person in relation to any given circumstance or situation is observed for evaluation to render an assessment and/ or conclusion. Methods to evaluate can include research, testing, interviews of various relevant persons, including the subject of the evaluation, and any material evidence available. Forensic evaluations are usually conducted for legal purposes, but other reasons are possible, such as providing a basis for a clinical treatment plan. Standardized reports are usually prepared and provided.

Pop/Political Climate – I devised this term as an expansion of the term "pop/political"(see Chapter 4 in Glossary). In context, referring to the climate metaphorically to indicate societal focus and fixation of the moment – *the daily special.*

Fake News – See Chapter 5 in Glossary.

$\left(^{\wedge}\text{-} `\right)$ – This is me winking at you.

Chapter 9

Faux Pas – It means blunder in French.

Fake News – See Chapter 5 in Glossary.

Fake – See Chapter 6 in Glossary.

Political Correctness – See Part I in Glossary.

Cognitive Dissonance – See Chapter 6 in Glossary.

Straw-man – See Chapter 4 in Glossary.

Red Meat – Colloquially to mean a political opponent's ravenous appetite to attack the opposition mercilessly. "Red meat" is a metaphor for intentionally or unintentionally serving-up anything the opponent, like a wild starving carnivore, relishes to attack. In context, Trump and what he says is "red meat" to his opposition.

Chapter 10

European Union – Organization of European countries established to govern common economic, social, and security policies.

The European Union was created by the Maastricht Treaty on November 1, 1993 to enhance political and economic integration by creating a single currency, the euro.

Tariff – Tax or duty imposed by a government on imported or exported goods.

National Security Council – A committee in the executive branch of government that advises the president on foreign, military, and national security. The National Security Council supervises the Central Intelligence Agency (CIA).

Skywriting – I can't remember the last time I saw skywriting, so I don't know if it's done any more. But it's a promotional marketing gimmick in which small aircraft write a "smoky, vapory" message in letters or other designs in the sky. Paraffin oil is mixed into the airplane's exhaust to create the effect.

"The Mob" – See Chapter 5 in Glossary.

Chapter 11

Twilight Zone – Iconic TV series, original run of five seasons from 1959 to 1964. Through a short-story, science fiction/fantasy genre, the series is an exploration of the human condition and commentary on how people cope with fear of the unknown. Plot twist and irony are a hallmark of the show.

Faux – It means *fake* in French.

Fake News – See Chapter 5 in Glossary.

Red Meat – See Chapter 9 in Glossary.

Street Cred – Short for "street credibility." Colloquially refers to having instincts and toughness in a "rough and tumble" world. Origins of the term refers to the acceptance and respect of people who live in poor city neighborhoods. In context, refers to the

battle-tested acknowledgment by political opponents and forti-
tude for taking on and winning political battles.

Part III

Ad hominem – See Chapter 4 in Glossary.

Fake – See Chapter 6 in Glossary.

Morality Play – Of medieval origins, plays presented for theatrical
entertainment, allegorically centered on a moral message. Themes
of God, righteousness, and evil are often depicted. The intent is
to evoke the audience to intense feelings. In context, referring
to any play arousing serious thought, reflection, and emotion
leading to a positive transformative state of understanding. This
can be related to political enlightenment.

Chapter 12

Mental Status Exam – Observational and behavioral findings
providing a profile of psychosocial functioning. These findings
are rendered in a standard formatted report referred to as a Mental
Status Exam.

Fake News – See Chapter 5 in Glossary.

Blood Sport – Used in this context colloquially to mean employing
an all-out rhetorical brutality against a political opponent
to accomplish its complete destruction. It's a win-at-all-cost
mentality. The media and press engage in blood sport when they
aggressively pile on for the "kill."

Tangentiality – In context to mental functioning, this refers to
diverging focus, thought, and speech from a starting point and
moving, often erratically, off point. This is considered a thought
dysfunction and can have a range of mild to extremely severe.

Composite Persona – I devised this term to identify a profile to use in an exercise construct. The exercise is based on a generalized profile of many persons who intersect along key character and purpose traits. In context, this is a composite of personalities in print- and broadcast-journalism. This provides a singular profile lending itself to reliable assumptions for the purpose of a limited scope of psychological forensics.

Reaction Formation – A dysfunctional psychological defense mechanism to cover-up something unacceptable by taking an opposite position. In context, with regard to politics and political personality figures, the psychological defense is to react by forming a concealment via false assertions. The mechanism does double duty by hiding and showing. It also self-aggrandizes, causing a false ego strength. An example would be a politician who has no problem with a wall for security on the U.S. Southern border. In fact they are in favor of it. But political correctness and fashion declare such a position is unacceptable, racist, and immoral. So, that politician takes a high profile leadership position to denounce a border wall. Reaction formations are complicated. (By the way, reaction formation is what's actually happening with the border wall issue, as well as so many other issues – *Reaction Formation* – that's a good title for my next book.)

Projective Identification – A dysfunctional psychological defense mechanism to project onto others undesirable and unwanted thoughts, feelings, and character traits you have, or fear you yourself have. This is often an unconscious process. In context, political polarization and contempt for persons who are of the political opposition causes susceptibility to projective identification in those with poor comprehension or dismissal of the psychological and motivational range of others.

Concrete Thinking (Concrete Reasoning, Concreteness) – This term, and variations of this term as in these three examples, refers to cognition (thinking process) that is literal, absent of abstraction. Without abstract cognitive comprehension of events and circumstances, any significance is lost and/or misunderstood. Literal and concrete thinking is primitive, immature, and unrefined. Such thinking lacks nuance and contextual appreciation. This is a flaw in understanding and reasoning. Conclusions drawn from concrete thinking are unreliable and possibly dangerous. The effects of concreteness can compound to a point of collapsing all rationality and sense of true meaning. In context, any journalist, pundit, or media personality's work-product affected by their concrete thinking is putting out unreliable flawed reporting, commentary, and opinion.

Fake – See Chapter 6 in Glossary.

Chapter 13

Political Psychosis – I appropriated this term from my editor's friend. But I get to say what it means. Political Psychosis is the irrationality and mental disturbance an individual or group of individuals shows in their susceptibility to the universe of politics – political governance, political personalities, and the political art/skill/degradation publically played out and reported or misreported by the media.

Pop/Political Arena – I devised this term as an expansion of the term "pop/political"(see Chapter 4 in Glossary). In context, referring to "arena" metaphorically and colloquially in the societal setting.

General Precursor – I devised this term to refer to existing maladapted psychological conditions that give root to extreme and irrational mental states, usually causing negative consequences. One's negative ideas and attitudes makes an individual vulnerable to coercive psychological distress. In context, political propaganda both takes advantage of and creates vulnerability. Such propaganda remakes vulnerability into victimhood and perpetuates the distress through message repetition.

Safe Spaces – A place or environment where a person or group of persons who identify with some category of people can retreat to for a feeling of comfort, support, and protection. Usually such places are provided at schools, particularly on college campuses.

Ego Muscle – I devised this term to refer to the essence of a person which can be considered their unique ego. In short, the ego is a person's conscious sense of self. The muscle part of the term is an index of the development, strength, and state of the ego. In context, in a world of ideological, philosophical, and political conflict, a person must have a base ego strength for stable functioning and general well-being.

Self-fulfilled, False Prophecy – I devised this phrase to refer to the psychological/cognitive complex in which one is compelled through psychological disorder to imagine with conviction about the existence, or future existence, of something that demonstrably does not exist and will not happen. Despite such fallacy, or oddly, even because of it, the individual is more convinced of the existence of what is not real.

Narcissistic – Excessive self-interest to the point other people don't matter or count for anything the narcissist cares about. Narcissistic traits can occur at times in non-pathological ways in an otherwise normal person. But as a personality disorder, narcissism is a serious psychopathology. Narcissists demand inordinate attention and admiration.

Primed for Catastrophe (PFC) – I devised this term to identify a predisposed condition for a specific focus of anxiety, depression, and distress. A person with this condition has expectations for disaster and misfortune that solid evidence to the contrary cannot affect. Such persons are emotionally invested in the specific doom and cannot be dissuaded otherwise. Erratic emotions and thought distortion are associated with PFC.

Pop/Political Culture – See Chapter 4 in Glossary.

Tongue-in-cheek – Colloquial phrase, meaning ironic or slyly humorous with subtle sarcasm. It references something said, written, or otherwise expressed.

Trigger Cue – Any person, event, or thing that ignites a specific psychological or emotional reaction. The trigger cue can have long-lasting effects; and if repeated can have a cumulative effect, worsening the reaction.

Collective Psychological Archetype – This term refers to the foundational essence of who we all are as a species and how we're all connected to each other from the beginning to now and as long as there's one of us left. An archetype is a quintessential representation of any given thing or concept. Psychological is of the psyche which is the human soul, mind, and spirit. Collective means all of us, anyone who ever was, is, and will ever be. So, the theory of collective psychological archetypes is the existence of themes and ideas that are constant and reoccurring through all generations and societies. There may be variations of the themes, but these themes exist in basic forms that do not need to be communicated, as was discovered by explorers who came upon previously unknown societies and found that similar meaningful themes, with nuanced abstractions, were known to these people too.

Pop/Political World – I devised this term as an expansion of the term "pop/political"(see Chapter 4 in Glossary). In context, referring to "world" metaphorically and colloquially in the societal setting.

Part IV

The Butterfly Effect – This refers to the far reaching effects of the slightest activity from one part of the world to effecting some activity as far away as the other side of the world. Like a butterfly flapping it's wings in Japan and causing, through infinite sequential effects, a car crash in Paris, France.

Chapter 14

Atrocities – Plural for atrocity. See Chapter 4 in Glossary.

"Break the fourth wall" – A theatrical technique or gag in movies, TV, and plays where a character in the story "steps out of the scene," acknowledges the audience as if they were always aware of the audience presence, speaks to the audience, or maybe just looks or gestures, and then returns their attention to the scene as if nothing happened. It's often played as if the gag is discretely between the character and the audience.

Sensibility Meter – I devised this term to refer to an intellectually internalized gauge of how sensible, rational, and smart you are in any given situation. It's a mental image and exercise to help you be aware of your thinking.

Morality Play – See Part III in Glossary.

Trilogy of Understanding – I devised this phrase to identify three core components to keen understanding, reasoning, and comprehension. Those components are common sense, uncommon sense, and wisdom.

Thought Ethos – I devised this term to refer to the combined make-up of philosophical, political, transcendence (could include religious, theological, or spiritual beliefs), outlook, worldview, intellectual, aesthetic, values, and humor that define in essence how a person has decided to be. It's a willful psychological/intellectual architecture of a person and "where they stand." It's a profile of a person's comprehension and understanding of things, and how they orient with it.

Ancient Times – In context of Western civilization, this broadly refers to Persian, Greek, Egyptian, Arab/Semitic, and Roman civilizations from at least a millennium Before the Common Era (BCE) or Before Christ (BC) – BCE and BC mean the same – to about fifth century Anno Domini (AD) – Anno Domini is Medieval Latin for "in the year of the Lord."

The Middle Ages – In context of Western civilization, this is a period of time from about fifth century AD to fifteenth century AD.

The Renaissance – In context of Western civilization, this is a period of time from about the fourteenth century to the seventeenth century, distinguished by a European surge of interest in art, literature, and science. "Renaissance" is French for "rebirth."

The Enlightenment – See Chapter 3 in Glossary.

The Industrial Revolution – See Part I in Glossary.

Chapter 15

Neanderthal – Colloquially and in context, I use this word pejoratively to underscore the un-evolved, mindless stupidity of people. Poor Neanderthals, they didn't do anything to deserve this disrespect. I'm sure there were Neanderthals with better sensibilities than many of our present day Homo sapiens.

Street Cred – See Chapter 11 in Glossary.

Bona Fides – A person's honesty, sincerity, and good faith intentions. Also, documentation and/or evidence of expertise and legitimacy. Credentials.

Dark Ages – I use the term to refer to the time between the fall of the Western Roman Empire and about two centuries before the age of the Renaissance. This period is also known as the Middle Ages. Currently, historians tend not to use the term "Dark Ages" as it's now considered to give the wrong connotation for this span of time. But for colloquial use and in context, the term connotes a period of time when enlightenment and vision for a specific aspect are rare or absent altogether. In this context, the aspect is politics.

Boogieman – An imaginary person or humanoid with evil supernatural powers. The idea of a boogieman can be symbolic; it can be thought of cynically with ridicule to poke fun at people's fears and paranoia. In context, in the political arena it's not enough to have a different opinion from your political opposition; a political adversary without integrity needs to fight an evil demon – a boogieman.

Political Correctness – See Part I in Glossary.

Bellwether – An indicator of trends. A predictor of something.

Market Correction – This refers to when a stock reaches high prices and then drops at least 10 percent. The drop is the correction. In context, I use the term metaphorically to refer to a simplified reason Trump was elected. A critical mass in politics, governance, and popular opinion converged at a high pitch to bring about a "correction" in the form of the "disruption" election of Trump.

Referendum – A single political question put to a general vote of the electorate.

Atrocity – See Chapter 4 in Glossary.

Concrete – See Chapter 8 in Glossary.

Trilogy of Understanding – See Chapter 14 in Glossary.

Chapter 16

Superdelegates – These are delegates created by political parties to function within their respective party. They are not created by the *Constitution* or Congress. These delegates are free to vote to nominate any candidate they choose, regardless of the democratic popular vote. The Democratic and Republican Parties both have superdelegates, but the percentage of these delegates is much higher and more influential in the Democratic Party. There has been much controversy over superdelegates in the Democratic Party having too much influence, and are thought by many to have corrupted the nomination process.

Binary – In context, there are only two options in a vote. There may be other candidates than just two, but it's usually obvious which two have a chance. Also, if you choose not to vote, which is a third choice, that's a vote for the one candidate you want the least. Effective voting is always a binary choice.

Chapter 17

No terms from this section.

Chapter 18

Pop/Political Culture – See Chapter 4 in Glossary.

Political Psychosis – See Chapter 13 in Glossary.

"Trump" Market Correction – See Chapter 15 in Glossary. In context, adding "Trump" to the term "market correction" is to label the metaphor specifically as a "Trump thing."

Ergo – It's one of those words like "alas" (see Chapter 5 in Glossary). It makes you feel like Shakespeare. It means therefore, consequently, so. "Ergo, there you are …"

Afterword

Stylings – See Chapter 1 in Glossary.

Unalienable Rights – See Chapter 2 in Glossary.

Cognitive Dissonance – See Chapter 6 in Glossary.

Concrete Thinking – See Chapter 8 in Glossary.

Projective Identification – See Chapter 12 in Glossary.

Quotes to Remember

THROUGHOUT THIS BOOK, I'VE BEEN DROPPING QUOTES. This section provides easy reference to some of them.

Introduction

1. *A republic, if you can keep it.* —Purportedly said by Benjamin Franklin.
2. *Freedom is never more than one generation away from extinction.* —Ronald Reagan

Part I

1. *We didn't start the fire. It was always burning since the world's been turning.* —Billy Joel
2. ... government *of the people, by the people, for the people* ... —Abraham Lincoln
3. ... *liberty and justice for all.* —From the Pledge of Allegiance, written by Francis Bellamy.

Chapter 1

1. ... *it has been said that democracy is the worst form of government except all those other forms that have been tried from time to time* ... —Winston Churchill

2. *It depends upon what the meaning of the word "is"... is.* —Bill Clinton

3. *No way around it, governance of some kind matters.* —Howard Asher

Chapter 2

1. *Only a virtuous people are capable of freedom. As nations become corrupt and vicious, they have more need of masters.* —Benjamin Franklin

2. *... Our Constitution was made only for a moral and religious people. It is wholly inadequate to the government of any other.* —John Adams

3. *Without virtue, happiness cannot be.* —Thomas Jefferson

4. *Human rights can only be assured among a virtuous people. The general government . . . can never be in danger of degenerating into a monarchy, an oligarchy, an aristocracy, or any despotic or oppressive form so long as there is any virtue in the body of the people.* —George Washington

Chapter 3

1. *If you don't know history, you won't get the jokes.* —A social studies teacher said this at parents night at my son's high school. I'm sorry I don't know his name, but his quote stayed with me all these years.

2. *Those who don't know history are doomed to repeat it.* —Many people have said something like this.

3. *History is repeated precisely because tyrants and the elites <u>know</u> their history.* —Howard Asher

4. Referring to this nation, ... *the last best hope on earth.* —Abraham Lincoln

5. Responding to the question: "What are you rebelling against?" *Whaddaya Got?* —Marlon Brando's character, Johnny Strabler, in *The Wild One.*

Chapter 4

1. *It's undeniable and unavoidable that African-Americans have a historical standing that is profoundly different than any other group in this nation. The atrocity of three hundred years of slavery and subsequent institutional victimization and humiliation cannot be erased.* —Howard Asher

Chapter 5

1. *If you want a picture of the future, imagine a boot stamping on a human face... forever.* —George Orwell, from his novel *1984.*
2. *Big Brother is watching you.* —George Orwell, from his novel *1984.*
3. *Do the right thing.* —Google's motto

Chapter 6

1. *I believe marriage is between a man and a woman. I am not in favor of gay marriage.* —Barack Obama
2. *Perception is reality.* —Lee Atwater
3. *The medium is the message.* —Marshall McLuhan
4. *Fashion is the issue.* —Howard Asher
5. *Fashion is something barbarous, for it produces innovation without reason and imitation without benefit.* —George Santayana
6. *... men may construe things after their fashion, clean from the purpose of the things themselves.* —William Shakespeare, from the play *Julius Caesar.*

Part II

1. *The elephant in the room is Donald Trump. Only with this elephant everybody's talking about it all the time.* —Howard Asher

Chapter 7

1. *Trump's election is going to be the biggest "fuck you" ever recorded in human history. And it will feel g-o-o-d.* —Michael Moore
2. *If the electorate allows a party, an office holder, or one who seeks office to take its votes for granted, our Republic won't survive.* —Howard Asher

Chapter 8

No quotes from this chapter.

Chapter 9

1. *Messaging is the "it" in leadership.* —Howard Asher
2. *... if you've got a business ... you didn't build that. Somebody else made that happen.* —Barack Obama
3. *You can put half of Trump supporters into what I call the basket of deplorables ...* —Hillary Clinton
4. *Make America great again ... Drain the swamp.* —Donald Trump

Chapter 10

1. *It's never the profession that ennobles. Rather, it's the practitioner that ennobles goodness, or on the other end of the spectrum, disgraces what should be good.* —Howard Asher

Chapter 11

1. *You're fired!* —Donald Trump

Part III

1. Who's crazy? *Anyone who can't be sensible when it's necessary.*
   —Howard Asher

Chapter 12

1. *By all evidence Trump is of sound mind. But he is quite a character.* —Howard Asher

Chapter 13

1. *The mass of men lead lives of quiet desperation.* —Henry David Thoreau
2. *But it is a characteristic of wisdom not to do desperate things.* —Henry David Thoreau
3. *The sky is falling!* —Chicken Little

Part IV

1. *Wherever you go, there you are.* —Most everyone has heard this saying. From my cursory research, it's origins are unknown or uncertain.
2. *The only thing you can't get away from is you.* —Howard Asher
3. *Living a sensible life is like a high-wire act. It's the art of maintaining the perfect balance between two fundamentally contradictory truths: it's not about you, and it's all about you.* —Howard Asher

Chapter 14

1. *God means good. And God is so good He only needs one "O."* —Howard Asher
2. Response to being publically validated – *Boy, if life were only like this.* —Alvy Singer, Woody Allen's character in *Annie Hall.*

3. After a round of golf the Dalai Lama gives a "tip" to his caddy telling him that he "will receive total consciousness on his death bed." Remarking on this "tip" – *So I got that going for me.* — Carl Spackler, Bill Murray's character in *Caddyshack*

4. *So, go forth and be wise ... and enlightened.* —Howard Asher

Chapter 15

1. *Never underestimate a person's intelligence or their stupidity.* —Howard Asher

2. *Imagine.* —John Lennon

3. *... the better angels of our nature.* —Abraham Lincoln

4. *You think racism can control me? Oh that don't stop me. That's an invisible wall.* —Kanye West

5. *Trump is a market correction!* —Howard Asher

Chapter 16

1. *Elections have consequences.* —Barack Obama

Chapter 17

1. *Have a good sense of humor.* —Howard Asher

Chapter 18

1. *The beat goes on ...* —Sonny and Cher

Afterword

1. *Please share this book with others. It can make a positive impression.* —Howard Asher

Acknowledgments

AS ALL AUTHORS DO IN THESE TIMES, I FORMED AN INTIMATE relationship with my laptop computer. To be precise, my used, ten-year-old, renovated 17" HP Compaq 6820s. This "guy" has been my constant companion throughout the production of the manuscript for *A Loose Grip*, as "he" is now, while I key punch this very word. I think it's just amazing! Everything that's in this book, the words, the research, contact information, everything came from these two rectangular pieces of plastic attached by hinges and connected to the Internet. I think it's remarkable what this day and age has brought us in technical advances, cultivated by the blessings of this Republic. I am grateful. Not to be left out, honorable mention goes to pads of sticky notes and a few Pilot G-2 gel pens. Thank you, you things. I couldn't have done it without you.

Now to the Homo sapiens: You, the reader, and I have had the great fortune to have the editing talents and skills of Marta Caylor. She's a gem! Marta is the perfect editor of the manuscript for this book. Her work on this project was meticulous and tireless. I clearly exploited her generosity, her time, her expertise, and her high standards. And even more for me, I have a dear friend in her. Thank you, Marta.

The way this book looks and reads is due to the brilliance of Ghislian Viau who designed the outside and insides of the look of *A Loose Grip*. He typeset what you are now reading (and, of course, the entire book). The importance of Ghislain's role in providing you a superior reading experience cannot be overstated. His design and typesetting company is *Creative Publishing Book Design*. If you are in need of such services, I recommend him highly.

My friend, Dr. Eric Belz, was a great support to me. He's a rocket scientist (more precisely he's a flight systems mathematician, but it's fun to say rocket scientist). Throughout the writing of the manuscript, Eric followed the progress. He read as I completed chapters and segments. We had many "bull sessions." And speaking of "bull sessions" my business associate, Suren Seron, was always there for me whenever I wanted help and guidance.

I have to thank the gang at *She & He* hair salon. I was welcomed into this group of guys and gals who ritually get together every Saturday morning at the salon for coffee, pastries, sometimes a haircut, and always a discussion/break-down of all things in life. The gang has taken a keen interest in *A Loose Grip* and have supported me throughout. Thank you Dennis Klempner, Steve Kasten, Jerry Beach, Robert "Bob" Campbell, Suki Barry, Barbara Yobs, Lucia Rutigliano, Mike O'Neal, April Schauer, Jerry Sriro, and Gary Hendison – the gang.

I want to thank Gene Agatep and Joel Ocosta. In their own respective ways, these guys were invaluable to me.

I began by acknowledging my laptop. If you have a laptop you gotta have a computer guy. My computer guy is Kyle Krupnick. Kyle thinks fast, talks fast, and trouble-shoots fast. He's a bit of a philosopher as well. (What computer guy isn't a philosopher?) Thanks Kyle. For websites and more, Glenn Hong is my "go to." His company is *B.I.T. Billionaires in Training*. There's a lot of work, skill, creativity, and functionality that went into the website. The web address is *aloosegrip*thebook.com. Please visit it and buy some books for family and friends.

My wife has stood by me through all the challenges life serves up. She's the best reason I wake up every day. Without her, my credentials, my expertise, and my life's work never would have happened.

And finally, I have to acknowledge you, the reader. If a tree falls in the forest and nobody is around to hear, does it make a noise? (I didn't make up that question, but I'm using it.) It most likely does make a noise. But it doesn't matter. Without you, the reader, this book doesn't matter. Thank you for taking your valuable time and spending it with me via *A Loose Grip. You make it matter!*

Notes

Introduction

1. Constitutional Convention (United States) - Wikipedia en.wilkipedia. org/wiki/Constitutional_Convention_(United_States).
2. Beeman, Richard R. "Perspectives on the Constitution: A Republic, If You Can Keep It." *National Constitution Center.*
3. Will The Great American Experiment Succeed? nccs.net/blogs/ our-ageless/.../will-the-great-american-experimemt-succeed.
4. Quotes on Liberty and Virtue - Institute for American Liberty liberty1. org/virtue.htm.
5. among these are Life, Liberty and the pursuit of Happiness - Founding founding.com/.../founding.../among-these-are-life-liberty-and-the-pursuit-of-happiness/ The Claremont Institute.
6. Object Relations Theory - Changing Minds changingminds.org > Disciplines > Psychoanalysis > Concepts.
7. Catharsis - Wikipedia en.wikipedia.org/wiki/Catharsis.
8. Constitution for the United States - We the People constitutionus.com/.
9. Brown, Elizabeth A.R. feudalism | Definition & History | Britannica. com britannica.com/topic/feudalism.
10. Welch, Scott D. Ronald Regan on the Constitution, Freedom ... - In Search of Liberty insearchofliberty.com/ronald-regan-on-the-constitution-freedom-liberty/. 16 August 2016.

Part I

1. Munro, André . republic | Definition, History, & Facts | Britannica.com britannica.com/topic/republic-government. 2018.
2. The Pledge of Allegiance - USHistory.org ushistory.org/documents/ pledge.htm. Independence Hall Association.
3. Exceptionalism dictionary definition | exceptionalism defined. Yourdictionary.com yourdictionary.com/exceptionalism.
4. Political Correctness | Encyclopedia. com encyclopedia.com/social-science-and-law/.../political-correctness. Thomson Gale. 2008.

5. Political Correctness - Wikipedia en.wikipedia.org/wiki/Political_correctness.

6. Sovereign - Wikipedia en.wikipedia.org/wiki/Sovereign.

7. Lloyd, James. Cicero - Ancient History Encyclopedia ancient.eu/Cicero/. 15 January 2013.

8. Moseley, Alexander. Locke, John: Political Philosophy | Internet Encyclopedia of Philosophy iep.utm.edu/locke-po/.

9. Shackleton, Robert. Montesquieu | Early Life, Career, Major Works, & Last Years ... britannica.com/biography/Montesquieu. 18 September 2018.

10. Delaney, James J. Rousseau, Jean Jacques | Internet Encyclopedia of Philosophy iep.utm.edu/rousseau/.

11. United States profile - Timeline - BBC News - BBC.com bbc.com/news/world-us-canada-16759233.

12. Brown, Cynthia Stokes. The Industrial Revolution (article) | Kahn Academy kahnacademy.org/partner-content/big.../bhp.../the-industrial-revolution.

13. The Alien and Sedition Acts ushistory.org.

14. Billy Joel - We Didn't Start the Fire Lyrics | Genius Lyrics genius.com > B > Billy Joel.

15. Constitution of the United States—A History | National Archives archives.gov/founding docs/more-perfect-union.

16. Bill of Rights - Bill of Rights Institute billofrightsinstitute.org/founding-documents/bill-of-rights/.

17. The Gettysburg Address rmc.library.cornell.edu/gettysburg/good_cause/transcript.htm.

Chapter 1

1. Groves, Steven. Why Does Sovereignty Matter to America? | The Heritage Foundation heritage.org/american-founders/.../why-does-sovereignty-matter-in-america. 3 December 2010.

2. "Democracy is the worst form of Government..." - Richard M. Langworth 26 June 2009. richardlangworth.com/worst-form-of-government. Web. 1 November 2018.

3. First Inaugural Address | National Archives Page last reviewed 15 August 1016. archives.gov/legislative/features/gw-inauguration.

4. Stromberg, Joseph. The Real Birth of American Democracy - *Smithsonian Magazine* 20 September 2018. smithsonianmg.com/smithsonian.../the-real-birth-of-american-democracy-83232825/.

5. Bernstein, Jamie. West Side Story westsidestory.com.

6. Romeo and Juliet | Folger Shakespeare Library folger.edu/romeo-and-juliet. Web. 1 November 2018.

7. Vito Corleone - Wikipedia en.wikipedia.com/wiki/Vito_Corleone.

8. Louisiana Purchase | Thomas Jefferson's Monticello monticello.org/site/jefferson/louisiana-purchase.

9. Lewis & Clark Expedition | National Archives Page last reviewed 25 April 2018. archives.gov/education/lessons/lewis-clark.

10. Lewis and Clark Expedition | History, Facts, & Map | Britannica.com britannica.com/event/Lewis-and Clark- Expedition.

11. Separation of powers | Legislative, Executive, Judicial ncsl.org/research/about-state-legislatures/separation-of-powers.aspx.

12. Noah, Timothy. Bill Clinton and the meaning of "is". *Slate* 13 September 1998. slate.com/news-and-politics/1998/09/bill-clinton-and-the-meaning-of-is.html.

13. White Only: Jim Crow in America-Separate Is Not Equal (Poll Tax) americanhistory.si.edu/1-segregated/white-only-1.html.

14. Healy, Gene. Remembering Nixon's Wage and Price Controls | Cato Institute *The DC Examiner* 16 August 2011. cato.org/publications/.../remembering-nixons-wage-and-price-controls.

15. The Dred Scott Decision [ushistory.org] ushistory.org/us/32a.asp.

Chapter 2

1. Willard, Wallace M. American Revolution | Causes, Battles, Aftermath, & Facts | Britannica.com britannica.com/ event/American-Revolution. 4 October 2018.

2. Kettler, Sara. The Founding Fathers: Who Were They Really? – Biography 4 July 2017 biography.com/news/founding-fathers-quotes-facts.

3. Duignan, Brian. Enlightenment | Definition, History & Facts | Britannica.com britannica.com/event/Enlightenment-European-history.

4. Editors of Encyclopedia Britannica. Declaration of Independence | History, Significance, & Text | Britannica.com britannica.com/topic/Declaration-of-Independence.

5. Strauss, Valerie. Are our rights 'inalienable or unalienable'? - The Washington Post washingtonpost.com/news/.../are-our-rights-inalienable-or-unalienable/. 4 July 2015.

6. Terms to Know - Center for Civic Education civiced.org/resources/curriculum/ 911-and-the-constitution/terms-to-know.

7. Articles of Confederation-Wikipedia en.wikipedia.org/wiki/Articles_of_Confederation.

8. The Original 13 States of the United States - ThoughtCo thoughtco.com > ... > American History > American Revolution.

9. Constitutional Convention of 1787 – See Introduction #1 in Notes.

10. The Bill of Rights – See Part I, #16 in Notes.

11. Constitution of the United States–A History | National Archives archives.gov/founding docs/more-perfect-union. Articles of Confederation.

12. Observing Constitution Day | National Archives archives.gov/education/lessons/constitution-day/ratification.html.

13. Separation of powers – See Chapter 1, #11 in Notes.

14. Old Testament | Definition & History | Britannica.com britannica.com/topic/Old-Testament.

15. New Testament | Definition & History | Britannica.com britannica.com/topic/New-Testament.

16. Judeo-Christian and Abrahamic Traditions in America-Oxford Research Encyclopedias religion.oxfordre.com/view/10.1093/acrefore/...001.../acrefore-9780199340378-e-425

17. What does Judeo-Christian mean? –The Dennis Prager Show dennisprager.com/what-does-judeo-christian-mean/.

18. In God we Trust - AllAboutHisory.org 2002. allabouthistory.org/in-god-we-trust.hlm.

19. Liberty - Wikipedia en.wikipedia.org/wiki/Liberty.

20. E Pluribus Unum - Wikipedia en,Wikipedia.org/wiki/E_pluribus_unum.

21. E Pluribus Unum-History of Motto Carried by Eagle on Great Seal greatseal.com/mottoes/unum.html.

22. Quotes on Liberty and Virtue – See Introduction, #4 in Notes.

Chapter 3

1. George Santayana - Wikiquote wikiquote.org/wiki/George_Santayana.

2. What Exactly is Mensa? How Smart Do You Have to Be to Join? people.howstuffworks.com > Culture > People > Education > Learning.

3. Sir William Wallace | Biography & Facts | Britannica.com btinnatica. com/biography/William-Wallace.

4. Bauer, Patricia. Braveheart | Plot, Cast, Awards, & Facts | Britannica. com britannica.com/topic/Braveheart.

5. Mel Gibson - Wikipedia en.wikipedia.org/wiki/Mel_Gibson.

6. Roman Empire-Ancient History Encyclopedia ancient.eu/ Roman_Empire/.

7. Mona Lisa - Portrait of Lisa Gherardini, wife of Francesco del – Louvre louvre.fr/…/ mona-lisa-portrait-lisa-gherardini-wife-of-francesco-del-giocondo.

8. Fabry, Merrill. Now You Know: Why Didn't People Smile in Old Photographs? | Time 28 November 2016. time.com > History > now you know.

9. Tooth decay first ravaged human society 15,000 years ago - USA Today usatoday.com/story/news/nation/2014/01/06/tooth-decay…/4307319/.

10. Indulgence | Roman Catholic | Britannica.com britannica.com/topic/ indulgence.

11. purgatory | Definition & History | Britannica.com britannica.com/ topic/purgatory-Roman-Catholicism.

12. Orta, Josep Palau. How Martin Luther Started a Religious Revolution 500 Years Ago 12 October 2017. nationalgeographic.com/…and…/ history-martin-luther-religious-revolution.

13. Reformation | History, Summary, & Reformers | Britannica.com britannica.com/event/Reformation.

14. Western Culture - ScienceDaily sciencedaily.com/terms/western_ culture.htm.

15. Breay, Claire, et al. Magna Carta an introduction-The British Library 28 July 2014. bl.uk/magna-carta/articles/magna-carta-an-introduction.

16. Stefansson, Vilhjalmur. What Is the Western Hemisphere? | Foreign Affairs January, 1941. foreignaffairs.com/articles/americas/1941-01…/ what-western-hemisphere.

17. Widmer, Ted. 'Last Best Hope'- *The New York Times* 30 November 2018. opinionattor.blogs.nytimes.com/2012/11/30/last-best-hope/.

18. Feudalism – See Introduction, #9 in Notes.

19. Zucker, Steven, et al. An introduction to the Protestant Reformation (article) | Khan Academy (Direct Relationship Doctrine) khanacacamemy.org/…reformation/…reformation/…/ an-introducton-to-the-protestant- reformation.
20. The Enlightenment – See Chapter 2, #3 in Notes.
21. Common Sense (pamphlet) - Wikipedia en.wikipedia.org/wiki/ Common_Sense_(pamphlet).
22. The Thirteen Colonies - Alpha History alphahistory.com/ americanrevolution/thirteen-colonies/.
23. Declaration of Independence – See Chapter 2, #4 in Notes.
24. *Constitution* – See Part I, #15 in Notes.
25. *The Wild One* (1953)-Filmsite filmsite.org/wild.html.
26. Marlon Brando Biography-life, family, children, school, mother, young … notablebiographies.com/Br-Ca/Brando-Marlon-html.
27. Boudreaux, Don. Most Ordinary Americans in 2016 Are Richer Than Was John D. Rockefeller Was in 1916. 20 February 2016. cafehayek. com/2016/02/40405.html.

Chapter 4

1. Jensen, Lisa. What Are Some Examples of Places Under Totalitarian Governments … theclassroom.com > Social Studies. 2018.
2. Haines, Gavin. Mapped: The world's most (and least) free countries – Telegraph telegraph.co.uk > Travel > News. 23 January 2018.
3. How Groups Voted in… *Roper Center for Public Opinion Research*. Cornell University.
4. Bositis, David A. "Blacks and the 2004 Democratic National Convention." Joint Center for Political and Economic Studies, Table 1, Presidential vote and party identification of black Americans, 1936–2000; p. 9. (As cited by Roper Center for Public Opinion Research).
5. Bositis, David A. "The Black Vote in 2004." Joint Center for Political and Economic Studies, 2005. (As cited by Roper Center for Public Research).
6. Casualties In The Civil War - Civil War Home civilwarhome.com/ casualties.htm. 1 November 2004.
7. Media Matters for America - Wikipedia enwikipedia.org/wiki/ Media_Matters_for_America.
8. Southern Poverty Law Center - Wikipedia enwikipedia.org/wiki/ Southern_Poverty_Law _Center.

9. MoveOn - Wikipedia enwikipedia.org/wiki/MoveOn.

10. Antifa (United States) - Wikipedia enwikipedia.org/wiki/
Antifa_(United_States).

11. Mulvaney: Mueller report 'not designed'
to exonerate Trump | *The Hill* thehill.
com/.../436615-mulvaney-mueller-report-not-designed-to-exonerate.

Chapter 5

1. The First Amendment. Constitution | US Law | LII / Legal Information
Institute. Cornell Law School.

2. Hate speech. Dictionary.com.

3. Defamation, Slander and Libel | Nolo.com nolo.com/legal.
encyclopedia/defamation-slander-libel.

4. Shakespeare, William. *The Tragedy of Hamlet, Prince of
Denmark*. Hamlet, Act III, Scene 1 :|: Open Source Shakespeare.
opensourceshakespeare.org. 2003-2018 George Mason University.

5. Lady Justice - Wikipedia en.wikipedia.org/wiki/Lady_Justice.

6. The Alien and Sedition Acts – See Part I, #13 in Notes.

7. McCullough, David. *John Adams*. New York: Simon and Shuster. 2001.

8. The American Presidency - National Museum of American History
americanhistory.si.edu/presidency/1b2.html (Presidential Oath).

9. Frank Capra - Wikipedia en.wikipedia.org/wiki/Frank-Capra.

10. *Mr. Smith Goes to Washington* (1939) - Filmsite filmsite.org/mrsm.html.
2010-2018.

11. James Stewart - Wikipedia en.wikipedia.org/wiki/James-Stewart.

12. Orwell, George. *1984* sparksnotes.com/lit/1984. 2018.

13. Hawkins, Stephen, et al. *Hidden Tribes: A Study of America's
Polarized Landscape*. New York: *More in Common*. October 2018.
moreincommon.com.

14. Mounk, Yascha. "America Strongly Dislikes PC Culture." *The Atlantic*.
10 October 2018.

15. Cato Institute. Poll: 71% of Americans Say Political Correctness Has
Silenced Discussions Society Needs to Have. cato.org. 31 October
2017.

16. Twitter - Wikipedia en.wikipedia.org/wiki/Twitter.

17. Facebook - Wikipedia en.wikipedia.org/wiki/Facebook.

18. YouTube - Wikipedia en.wikipedia.org/wiki/YouTube.

19. Google - Wikipedia en.wikipedia.org/wiki/Google.

20. Molina, Brett. Shadow Banning: What is it, and why is Trump talking about it on Twitter (sic). *USA Today* 26 July 2018. usatoday.com/story/tech/nation-now/2018/.../shadow.../842368002/.

21. Nolan, Lucas. Twitter Censorship: What is Shadow Banning? | Breitbart breitbart.com/tech/2018/01/.../twitter-censorship-what-is-shadow-banning... 11 January 2018.

22. Orwell, George. *Animal Farm*. eBooks@Adelaide. The University of Adelaide Library 22 February 2016.

23. Orwell, George. *Animal Farm* sparksnotes.com/lit/animalfarm. 2018.

24. Thierer, Adam. *Why the Fairness Doctrine is Anything But Fair.* The Heritage Foundation. heritage.org/government. 29 October 1993.

Chapter 6

1. President Barack Obama's shifting stance on gay marriage | PolitiFact. 11 May 2012. politifact.com/.../statements/.../11/...obama/president-barack-obama-shift-gay-marriage/.

2. Flashback: Biden's 2012 Endorsement of Same-Sex Marriage nbcnews.com/meet-the-press/.../flashback-bidens-2012-endorsement-of-same-sex-marriage.

3. When Truth is Blurred by Lies and Misinformation Perception ... - Funny (perception is reality) 2 May 2013. me.me/.../when-truth-is-blurred- by-lies-and-misinformation-perception-becomes...

4. Kelner, Simon. Perception is reality: The facts won't matter in next year's general election 30 October 2014. independent.co.uk > Voices > Comment.

5. The Medium is the Message by Marshall McLuhan – Eudaimonia ... 7 December 2016. *medium.com/@obtaineudaimonia/the-medium-is-the-message-by-marshall-mcluhan-* 8b5d0a9d42...

6. JFK Was a Political Conservative | TIME.com ideas.time.com/2013/10/14/jfk-was-a-political-conservative/.

7. JFK's Lasting Economic Legacy: Lower Tax Rates : NPR npr.org/2013/11/14/.../jfk-lasting-economic-legacy-lower-tax-rates.

8. Cherry, Kendra. What is Cognitive Dissonance? – Verywell Mind 21 September 2018. verywellmind.com > Psychology > Theories > Cognitive Psychology.

9. George Santayana - Wikiquote en.wikiquote.org/wiki/George_Santayana.

10. Julius Caesar, Act 1, Scene 3, :|: Open Source Shakespeare opensourceshakespeare.org/.../play_view.php?... juliuscaesar&Act=1&Se…

Part II

1. Donald Trump - Wikipedia en.wikipedia.org/wiki/Donald Trump. Web. 15 August 2018.

Chapter 7

1. YouTube. "Michael Moore Explains Why Trump Will Win." Online video clip. *YouTube*, 24 October 2016.

2. Brexit - Wikipedia enwikipedia.org/wiki/Brexit

Chapter 8

1. Trump signs VA Mission Act into law, though funding questions remain 6 June 2018. federalnewsradio.com/ veterans-affairs/.../ trump-signs-va-mission-act-into-law-t…

2. Bennett, Geoff. Congress Passes VA Accountability And Whistleblower Protection Act… NPR 13 June 2017. npr.org/.../ congress-passes-bill-to-increase-accountability-among-va-emplo…

Chapter 9

1. YouTube. "Bitter-People-Clinging-to-Guns Speech." Online video clip. *YouTube*, 6 April 2008.

2. YouTube. "If You've Got A Business, You Didn't Build That." Online video clip. *YouTube*, 16 July 2012.

3. YouTube. "Clinton: Trump Supporters in Basket of Deplorables…." Online video clip. *YouTube*, 9 September 2012.

4. Andersen, Hans C. "The Emperor's New Clothes." The Hans Christian Andersen Center, Department for the Study of Culture at the SDU 11 August 2011.

Chapter 10

1. News – Google Chrome. Dictionary.

2. Cassleman, Ben. "Economy Hits a High Note, and Trump Takes a Bow." *The New York Times* 27 July 2018 Published: Page A1. *The New York Times Website.*

3. YouTube. "Breaking News Headlines AC 369." Online video clip. *YouTube*, 27 July 2018.

4. YouTube. "CNN Tonight with Don Lemon Today [7/27/2018] Breaking News Tonight Today July 27, 2018." Online video clip. *YouTube*, 27 July 2018.

5. YouTube. "The Rachel Maddow Shown 7/27/18 MSNBC Breaking News July, 27, 2018." Online video clip. *YouTube*, 27 July 2018.

6. "Journalism." Google Chrome. Dictionary.

7. Gill, Kathy. What is the Fourth Estate? - *ThoughtCo*. thoughtco.com > Humanities > Issues > U.S. Government. 17 April 2018.

Chapter 11

1. The Apprentice (U.S. TV series) - Wikipedia en.wikipedia.org/wiki/The_Apprentice_(U.S._TV_sertes).

2. The Celebrity Apprentice - Wikipedia en.wikipedia.org/wiki/The_Celeberty_ Apprentice.

3. Aggeler, Madeleine. We Finally Know Why Omarosa Was Fired From the White House. *The Cut*. thecut.com/.../we-finally-know-why-omarosa-was-fired-from-the-white-house 13 February 2018.

4. Manigault-Stallworth, Omarosa. *The Bitch Switch: Knowing How to Turn It on and Off*. Los Angeles: Phoenix Press. 2008.

5. Trump, Donald with Schwartz, Tony. *The Art of the Deal*. New York: Ballantine Books. 1987.

6. Jack Benny – Biography - IMBd. Imbd.com/name/nm0000912/bio.

7. National Unemployment Rate - Bureau of Labor Statistics Data. data.bls.gov/timeseries/LNS14000000. 24 October 2018.

8. Don't Look Now, But Minority Unemployment Is At Record Lows Under Trump. *Investor's Business Daily* 5 January 2018. investors.com/.../dont-look-now-but-minority-unemployment-is-at-recor...

Part III

1. 25th Amendment. Constitution | US Law | LII / Legal Information Institute Cornell Law School.

2. Lee, Bandy, et al. *The Dangerous Case of Donald Trump*. New York: Thomas Dunne Books, St. Martin's Press. October 2017.

3. Personal and Political Papers of Barry M. Goldwater 1880s-2008. Arizona Archives Online. arizonaarchivesonline.org/xtf/view?docld=ead/asu/goldwater...barry%20goldwater. (Goldwater v. Ginzburg).

4. The Principles of Medical Ethics, American Psychiatric Association vpul.upenn.edu/caps/files/ethics-principlesMD-2010_1344281377.pdf. (Section 7.3).

5. Levin, Aaron. Goldwater Rule - American Psychiatric Association psychiatry.org/newsroom/goldwater-rule. 25 August 2018.

6. Transcript of the Duty to Warn Conference Yale School of Medical April 20, 2017. us.macmillan .com/static/duty-to-warn-conference-transcript.pdf.
7. A Duty To Warn-Mental Health Professionals Warning the Nation. adutytowarn.org/. 2018.
8. Morality play | dramatic genre | Britannica.com britannica.com/art/moralty-play-dramatic-genre.

Chapter 12

1. Mental Status Examination: Psychiatry and Behavioral Sciences med. enr.edu/psychiatry/education/resources/mental-status-examination.
2. Blood Sport | Definition of Blood Sport by Merriam-Webster merriam-webster.com/dictionary/blood%20sport.
3. YouTube. "Word for Word: President Trump on Judge Kavanaugh's Drinking Habits (C-SPAN)." Online video clip. *YouTube*, 1 October 2018.
4. Remarks by President Trump in Meeting with Republican Congressional Leadership 5 September 2018. whitehouse.gov/.../remarks-president-trump-meeting-republican-congress...
5. Don Lemon rips Trump over personal attack - YouTube 6 August 2018. Online video clip. *YouTube*. youtube.com/watch?v=tzZGuFJTs1l. Web. 24 October 2018.
6. Valmond, Sebastian. CNN's Ana Navarro Compares Trump To Someone Who Has Alzheimer's Or Dementia. Published on 30 November 2017. Online video clip. *YouTube*.
7. U.S. Electoral College, Official - What is the Electoral College? archives.gov/federal-register/electoral-college/about.html.
8. Ana Navarro great rant about Trump's tweeting-YouTube 29 June 2018. Online video clip. *YouTube*. youtube.com/watch?v=WhhXtCkt9CE.
9. Reaction Formation - Changing Minds changingminds.org > Explanations > Behaviors > Coping.
10. Lady Doth Protest too Much - Meaning and Usage - Literary Devices. (from Shakespeare's Hamlet, Act 3, Scene 2). literarydevices.net/lady-doth-protest-too-much/.
11. What is projective identification? - Drs-Oleary drs-oleary.com/Projective_Identification.htm.
12. Rachel Maddow | MSNBC - YouTube 26 October 2018. Online video clip. *YouTube*. youtube.com/watch?v=NidkK2rVSFs.

13. Concrete Thinking - Good Therapy goodtherapy.org > PsychPedia A-G.

14. Trump's off- the-rails news conference on Charlottesville response 15 August 2017. Online video clip. Global News. *YouTube*.

15. This is how America feels about Trump – Politico 24 October 2018. politico.com/interactive/2017/politico-morning-consult-poll.

Chapter 13

1. Definition of Psychosis - MedicineNet medicinenet.com/script/main/art.asp?articlekey=5110.

2. Derangement definition and meaning | Collins English Dictionary collinsenglishdictionary.com/us/dictionary/English/derangement.

3. Hysteria | Definition of Hysteria by Merriam-Webster merriam-webster.com/dictionary/hysteria.

4. Anxiety | Definition of Anxiety by Merriam-Webster merriam-webster.com/dictionary/anxiety.

5. Definition of Delusion - MedicineNet medicinenet.com/scrit/main/art.asp?articlekey=26290.

6. What is Psychological Distress? - Definition & Symptoms - Video ... Study.com/academy/.../what-is-psychological-distress-definition-lesson-quiz-html.

7. Dysfunction | Definition of Dysfunction by Merriam-Webster merriam-webster.com/dictionary/dysfunction.

8. Ideation | definition of ideation by Medical dictionary medical-dictionary.thefreedictionary.com/ideation.

9. Syndrome | Definition of Syndrome by Merriam-Webster merriam-webster.com/dictionary/syndrome.

10. Paranoia | Definition, Types, & Facts | Britannica.com britannica.com/science/paranoia.

11. Henry David Thoreau - Poet, Philosopher, Journalist – Biography 2 April 2014. biography.com/people/henry-david-thoreau-9506784.

12. 1124. Henry David Thoreau (1817-62). Respectfully Quoted: A Dictionary of Quotations. 1989. bartleby.com/73/1124.html.

13. Furedi, Frank. Campuses are breaking apart into 'safe spaces' – *Los Angeles Times* 5 January 2017. latimes.com/opinion/op-ed/la-oe-furedi-safe-space-20170105-story.html.

14. An Overview of the American's With Disabilities Act | ADA National Network. 2017. adata.org/factsheet/ADA-overview.

15. *The Dangerous Case of Donald Trump* – See Part III, #2 in Notes.
16. Axis I – PSYweb psyweb.com/DSM_IV/jsp/Axis_I.jsp.
17. *Diagnostic and Statistical Manual* (DSM) Overview - Verywell Mind verywellmind.com > Psychology > Psychotherapy.
18. Krauthammer, Charles. "Bush Derangement Syndrome." *Town Hall* 5 December 2003.
19. Whitley, David. Streisand gets plump, blames Trump – *Orlando Sentinel* orlandosentinel.com/.../os-ae-streisand-trump-david-whitlet-1301-story.html.
20. Chicken Little - Story - WorldStory.Net 2005. worldstory.net/en/stories/chicken_little.html.
21. Aarne-Thompson classification system. Open Access articles | Omics International.

Part IV
No notes in this section.

Chapter 14
1. *In God We Trust* – See Chapter 2, #18 in Notes.
2. Woody Allen - Wikipedia enwikipedia.org/wiki/ Woody_Allen.
3. Film Forum - Annie Hall filmforum.org/film/annie-hall-2017.
4. Diane Keaton - Wikipedia enwikipedia.org/wiki/Diane_Keaton.
5. Woody Allen meets Marshall McLuhan - *YouTube*. youtube.com/?watchv=sXJ8tKRIW3E.
6. Who is Marshall McLuhan? - The Estate of Marshall McLuhan 2018. marshallmcluhan.com/biography.
7. Mr. Potato Head - Wikipedia en.wikipedia.org/wiki/Mr._Potato_Head.
8. History of Western civilization before AD 500 - Wikipedia en.wikipedia.org/wiki/History_of_Western_civilization_before_AD_500.
9. Middle Ages | Definition & Facts | Britannica.com britannica.com/event/Middle-Ages.
10. Renaissance | Definition of Renaissance by Merriam-Webster merriam-webster.com/dictionary/renaissance.
11. The Enlightenment – See Chapter 2, #3 in Notes.
12. The Industrial Revolution – See Part I, #12 in Notes.
13. Bill Murray - Wikipedia en.wikipedia.org/wiki/Bill-Murray.
14. *Caddyshack* (1979) | The Film Spectrum thefilmspectrum.com/?p=21062.

15. Dalai Lama - Wikipedia en.wikipedia.org/wiki/Dalai-Lama.

Chapter 15

1. Imagine (John Lennon song) - Wikipedia en.wikipedia.org/wiki/ imagine_(John_Lennon_song).

2. Great inaugural addresses: Abraham Lincoln's two speeches … constitutionalcenter.org/blog/ great-inaugural-speeches-abraham-lincoln/.

3. Transcript: Kanye West in the Oval Office - CNNPolitics - CNN.com cnn.com/2018/10/11/politics/kanye-west-oval-office/index.html.

4. I Have a Dream - Martin Luther King, Jr., Research and Education Institute kinginstitute.stanford.edu/ king…/i-have-a-dream-delivered-march-washi…

5. Skelley, Geoffrey. Just How Many Obama 2012-Trump 2016 Voters Where There? 1 June 2017. resmussenreports.com/…/ just_how_many_obama_2012_trump_2016_voters_were_there?

6. Executive Order 9066: The President Authorizes Japanese Relocation historymatters.gmu.edu/d/5154

7. The History Place - Genocide in the 20th Century: Stalin's Forced Famine 1932-1933 historyplace.com/worldhistory/genocide/stalin.htm.

8. The History Place - Genocide in the 20th Century: The Nazi Holocaust 1938-1945 historyplace.com/worldhistory/genocide/holocaust.htm.

9. The History Place - Genocide in the 20th Century: Pol Pot in Cambodia 1975-1979 historyplace.com/worldhistory/genocide/pol-pot.htm.

10. Holzer, Harold. Stop the Presses: Lincoln Suppresses Journalism | HistoryNet 20 February 2018. historynet.com/stop-the-presses-lincoln-suppresses-journalism.htm.

11. The Alien and Sedition Acts, John Adams – See Part I, #13, Chapter 5, #7, in Notes.

12. Amadeo, Kimberly. Trump Tax Plan: How it Affects You. Tax Chart - The Balance updated 25 October 2018. thebalance.com/ trump-s-tax-plan-how-it-affects-you-4113968.

13. Pickrell, Ryan. Here Are The 17 Prisoners Trump Has Freed Since He Took Office 27 May 2018. dailycaller.com/2018/05/27/ president-trump-freed-17-prisoners/.

14. Friedman, Uri. Why Trumps North Korea Summit Was a Success-*The Atlantic* 6 July 2018. theatlantic.com/international/archive/2018/07/…/ north-korea/564359/.

15. Trump signs legislation, VA Mission Act – See Chapter 8, #1 in Notes.

16. Trump signs legislation, VA Accountability and Whistleblower Protection Act – See Chapter 8, #2 in Notes.

17. Moon, Emily. Trump Signs the Water Infrastructure Act - Pacific Standard 23 October 2018. psmag.com/news/trump-signs-the-2018-water-infrastructure-act.

18. How Flint's Water Crisis Happened, And, Why It Isn't Over | Here & Now wbur.org/hereandnow/2018/07/10/flint-water-crisis-poisoned-city.

19. Schwartz, Ian. Maher: I'm "Hoping" For "A Crashing Economy" So We Can Get Rid Of Trump 9 June 2018. realclearpolitics.com/.../maher-im-hoping-for-a-crashing-economy-so-we-can-get-rid-of-trump.

20. Pax on both houses: Einstein: "The Majority Of The Stupid Is Invincible … paxonbothhouses.blogspot.com/2013/11/einstein-majority-of-stupid-is.html.

Chapter 16

1. Wiblin, Robin. How much is one vote worth? - 80,000 Hours 4 November 2016 80000hours.org > Blog.

2. Rock the Vote - Wikipedia en.wikipedia.org/wiki/Rock_the_Vote.

3. Mutual Aid Societies - P2P foundation wiki.p2pfoundation.net/Mutual_Aid_Societies.

4. Opinion | Eric Cantor: What the Obama Presidency Looked like to the Opposition 14 January 2017. nytimes.com/.../eric-cantor-what-the-obama-presidency-looked-like-to-the-opposition.

5. Wolf, Z. Byron. Could Sanders have won primary that wasn't 'rigged'? – CNNPolitics 4 November 2017. cnn.com/2017/11/04/politics-bernie-sanders-2016-election…/index.html.

Chapter 17

No notes in this section.

Chapter 18

1. Mueller Report – See Chapter 4, #11 in Notes.

2. Sonny & Cher - Wikipedia enwikipedia.org/wiki/Sonny_%26_Cher.

3. "Trump" Market Correction – See Chapter 15 in Glossary.

Afterword

1. Cognitive Dissonance – See Chapter 6, #8 in Notes.

2. Projective Identification – See Chapter 12, #11 in Notes.

Glossary Notes

Introduction

1. Experiment – See Introduction, #3 in Notes.
2. Object Relations Theory – See Introduction, #6 in Notes.
3. Catharsis – See Introduction, #7 in Notes.
4. Feudalism – See Introduction, #9 in Notes.

Part I

1. Exceptionalism – See Part I, #3 in Notes.
2. Jingoistic definition and meaning | Collins English Dictionary collinsdictionary.com/us/dictionary/english/jingoistic.
3. Jingoism | Definition of Jingoism by Merriam-Webster merriam-webster.com/dictionary/jingoism.
4. Political Correctness – See Part I, #4, #5 in Notes.
5. "The Experiment" – See Introduction, #3 in Notes.
6. Industrial Revolution – See Part I, #12 in Notes.
7. The Alien and Sedition Acts – See Part I, #13 in Notes.

Chapter 1

1. Sovereignty | Definition of Sovereignty by Merriam-Webster merriam-webster.com/dictionary/sovereignty.
2. Stylings – definition of stylings by The Free Dictionary thefreedictionary.com/stylings.
3. Vito Corleone – See Chapter 1, #7 in Notes.
4. Fire sale-Wikipedia en.wikipeidia.org/wiki/Fire_sale.
5. Louisiana Purchase | Thomas Jefferson's Monticello monticello.org/site/jefferson/louisiana-purchase.
6. Treaty-Lingo-Kabuki – I devised this term. See Chapter 1 in Glossary.
7. Is – See Chapter 1, #12 in Notes.

Chapter 2

1. The Enlightenment – See Chapter 2, #3 in Notes.
2. Unalienable Rights – See Chapter 2, #5 in Notes.
3. Factoid | Definition of Factoid by Merriam-Webster merriam-webster.com/dictionary/factoid.
4. Terms to Know - Center for Civic Education civiced.org/curriculum/911-and-the-constitution/terms-to-know.
5. *E Pluribus Unum* – See Chapter 2, #20, #21 in Notes.

Chapter 3

1. Mensa – See Chapter 3, #2 in Notes.
2. Mona Lisa – See Chapter 3, #7 in Notes.
3. Indulgences – See Chapter 3, #10 in Notes.
4. *Magna Carta* – See Chapter 3, #15 in Notes.
5. Feudalism – See Introduction, #9 in Notes.
6. Direct Relationship Doctrine – See Chapter 3, #19 in Notes.
7. The Reformation – See Chapter 3, #13 in Notes.
8. The Enlightenment – See Chapter 2, #3 in Notes.
9. *Common Sense* – See Chapter 3, #21 in Notes.
10. "The Experiment" – See Introduction, #3 in Notes.
11. Vassal | Definition of Vassal by Merriam-Webster merriamwebstert. com/dictionary/vassal.
12. Grievance Class – I devised this term. See Chapter 3 in Glossary.

Chapter 4

1. Totalitarian | Definition of Totalitarianism by Merriam-Webster merriam-webster.com/dictionary/totalitarian.
2. Ad Hominem | Definition of Ad Hominem by Merriam-Webster merriam-webster.com/dictionary/ad%20hominem.
3. Your logical fallacy is strawman yourlogicalfallacyis.com/strawman.
4. "Atrocity." Google Chrome. Dictionary.
5. Dark Divides – See Chapter 4 in Glossary.
6. Toxic Divide of Destruction – See Chapter 4 in Glossary.
7. Pop/Political – I devised this term. See Chapter 4 in Glossary.
8. Pop/Political Culture – I devised this term. See Chapter 4 in Glossary.

Chapter 5

1. Abridging – Definition of abridging by The Free Dictionary thefreedictionary.com/abridging.
2. Sovereign Nation – See Chapter 1, #1 in Glossary Notes.
3. Exceptionalism – See Part I, #3 in Notes.
4. Interesting Facts about Lady Justice: A Legal Symbol of American Justice! interestingfacts.tv/.../ interesting-facts-about-lady-justice-a-legal-symbol-of-ame…
5. Unalienable Rights – See Chapter 2, #5 in Notes.
6. The Alien and Sedition Acts – See Part I, #13 in Notes.
7. alas | Definition of alas in English by Oxford Dictionaries en.oxforddictionaries.com/definition/alas.

8. Political Correct – See Part I, #4, #5 in Notes.
9. Fake News – See Chapter 5 in Glossary.
10. Gestapo | Nazi political police | Britannica.com. Updated 20 September 2018. bitannica.com/topic/Gestapo.
11. "The Mob" – See Chapter 5 in Glossary.
12. De facto - Wikipedia enwkipedia.org/wiki/De_facto.
13. De Facto | Definition by Merriam-Webster merriam-webster.com/dictionary/de%20facto.
14. Book burning - Wikipedia enwikipedia.org/wiki/Book_burning.

Chapter 6
1. Fake | Definition of Fake by Merriam-Webster merriam-webster.com/dictionary/fake.
2. Fashion Tribe – I devised this term. See Chapter 6 in Glossary.
3. Fashion Warrior – I devised this term. See Chapter 6 in Glossary.
4. Non Sequitur | Definition of Non Sequitur by Merriam-Webster merriam-webster.com/dictionary/non%20sequitur.
5. Rorschachian – Rorschach Inkblot Test - Psych Central psychcental.com/lib/rorschach_inkblot_ test/.
6. Ethos | Definition of Ethos by Merriam-Webster merriam-webster.com/dictionary/ethos.
7. Cognitive Dissonance – See Chapter 6, #8 in Notes.

Part II
No terms in this section.

Chapter 7
1. Tectonic | Definition of Tectonic by Merriam-Webster merriam-webster.com/dictionary/tectonic.
2. Litmus Test | Definition of Litmus Test by Merriam-Webster merriam-webster.com/dictionary/litmus%20test.
3. Reactionary |Definition of Reactionary by Merriam-Webster merriam-webster.com/dictionary/reactionary.
4. U.S. Electoral College Official - What is the Electoral College? archives.gov/federal-register/electoral-college/about.html.
5. Amorphous | Definition of Amorphous by Merriam-Webster merriam-webster.com/dictionary/amorphous.
6. Fake – See Chapter 6, #1 in Glossary Notes.
7. Brexit – See Chapter 7, #2 in Notes.

8. Repo | Definition of Repo by Merriam-Webster merriam-webster.com/dictionary/repo.
9. Ad hominem – See Chapter 4, # 2 in Glossary Notes.
10. Cathartically – Adverb of catharsis. See Introduction, #7 in Notes.
11. Cognitive Dissonance – See Chapter 6, #8 in Notes.
12. Double Cognitive Dissonance – See Chapter 6, #8 in Notes. In context, I added the "double" to refer to the compounding of the cognitive dissonance process.

Chapter 8
1. Fake – See Chapter 6, #1 in Glossary Notes.
2. Tyler Ward, Jane. What is forensic psychology? - American Psychological Association apa.org/ed/precollege/psn/2013/09/forensic-psychology.aspx.
3. Pop/Political – I devised this term. See Chapter 4 in Glossary.
4. Pop/Political Climate – I devised this term. See Chapter 8 in Glossary.
5. Fake News – See Chapter 5 in Glossary.
6. Winking – It's a friendly gesture. It conveys connection and maybe amusing irony.

Chapter 9
1. *Faux Pas* – Google Chrome. Dictionary.
2. Fake News – See Chapter 5 in Glossary.
3. Fake – See Chapter 6, #1 in Glossary Notes.
4. Political Correctness – See Part I, #4, #5 in Notes.
5. Cognitive Dissonance – See Chapter 6, # 8 in Notes.
6. Straw man - Wikipedia en.wikipedia.org/wiki/Straw_man
7. Red Meat | Definition of Red Meat by Merriam-Webster merriam-webster.com/dictionary/red%20meat.

Chapter 10
1. Gabel, Matthew J. European Union | Definition, Purpose, History, & Members | Britannica.com britannic.com/topic/European-Union.
2. Tariff | Definition of Tariff by Merriam-Webster merriam-webster.com/dictionary/tariff.
3. National Security Council - Dictionary Definition : Vocabulary.com vocabulary.com/dictionary/National%20Security%20Council.
4. How does skywriting and skytyping work? Everyday Mysteries: Fun … loc.gov/rr/scitech/mysteries/skywriting.html.
5. "The Mob" – See Chapter 5 in Glossary.

Chapter 11

1. LaFrance, Adrienne. How The Twilight Zone Predicted Our Paranoid Present - *The Atlantic* 31 December 2013. theatlantic.com/entertainment/archive/2013/...twilight-zone.../282700/.
2. *Faux* – Google Chrome. Dictionary.
3. Fake News – See Chapter 5 in Glossary.
4. Red Meat – See Chapter 9, #7 in Glossary Notes.
5. Street Cred | Definition of Street Cred by Merriam-Webster merrian-webster.com/dictionary/street%20cred.

Part III

1. Ad hominem – See Chapter 4, # 2 in Glossary Notes.
2. Fake – See Chapter 6, #1 in Glossary Notes.
3. Morality play – See Part III, #8 in Notes.

Chapter 12

1. Mental Status Examination: Psychiatry and Behavioral Sciences ... med.unr.edu/psychiatry/education/resources/mental-status-examination.
2. Fake News – See Chapter 5 in Glossary.
3. Blood Sport | Definition of Blood Sport by Merriam-Webster merriam-webster.com/dictionary/blood%20sport.
4. Tangentiality - an overview | ScienceDirect Topics sciencedirect.com/topics/medicine-and-dentistry/tangentiality.
5. Composite Persona – I devised this term. See Chapter 12 in Glossary.
6. Reaction Formation – See Chapter 12, #9 in Notes.
7. Projective Identification – See Chapter 12, #11 in Notes.
8. Concrete Thinking – See Chapter 12, #13 in Notes.
9. Fake – See Chapter 6, #1 in Glossary Notes.

Chapter 13

1. Political Psychosis – See Chapter 13 in Glossary.
2. Pop/Political Arena – I devised this term. See Chapter 13 in Glossary.
3. Precursor | definition in the Cambridge English Dictionary dictionary. cambridge.org/us/dictionary/english/precursor.
4. Safe Space | Definition of Safe Space by Merriam-Webster merriam-webster.com/dictionary/safe%20space.
5. Ego | Definition of Ego by Merriam-Webster merriam-webster.com/dictionary/ego.
6. Self-fulfilled, False Prophecy – I devised this term. See Chapter 13 in Glossary.

7. Narcissistic personality disorder - Symptoms and causes - Mayo Clinic mayoclinic.org/deseases-conditions/narcissistic...causes/syc-20366662.
8. Primed for Catastrophe (PFC) – I devised this term. See Chapter 13 in Glossary.
9. Pop/Political Culture – I devised this term. See Chapter 4 in Glossary.
10. Urban Dictionary: tongue in cheek urbandictionary.com/define. php?term=tongue%20in%20cheek.
11. The Psychology of Triggers and How They Affect Mental Health goodtherapy.org > PsychPedia R-Z.
12. Cherry, Kendra. The 4 Major Jungians Archetypes - VeryWell Mind 13 June 2018. verywellmind.com > Psychology > Theories > Personality Psychology.
13. Pop/Political World – I devised this term. See Chapter 13 in Glossary.

Part IV
1. Understanding the Butterfly Effect | American Scientist americanscientist.org/article/understanding_the _butterfly_effect.

Chapter 14
1. Atrocities – Plural for atrocity. See Chapter 4, #4 in Glossary Notes.
2. Break the fourth wall - Idioms by The Free Dictionary idioms. thefreedictionary.com /break+the+fourth+wall.
3. Sensibility Meter – I devised this term. See Chapter 14 in Glossary.
4. Morality Play – See Part III, #8 in Notes.
5. Trilogy of Understanding – I devised this term. See Chapter 14 in Glossary.
6. Thought Ethos – I devised this term. See Chapter 14 in Glossary.
7. Ancient Times – See Chapter 14, #6 in Notes.
8. The Middle Ages – See Chapter 14, #7 in Notes.
9. The Renaissance – See Chapter 14, #8 in Notes.
10. The Enlightenment – See Chapter 2, #3 in Notes.
11. The Industrial Revolution – See Part I, #12 in Notes.

Chapter 15
1. Neanderthal | Definition of Neanderthal by Merriam-Webster merriam-webster.com/dictionary/Neanderthal.
2. Street Cred – See Chapter 11, #5 in Glossary Notes.
3. Bona Fides | Definition of Bona Fifes by Merriam-Webster merriam-webster.com/dictionary/bona%20fides.

4. The Dark Ages-AllAboutHistory.org allabouthistory.org/the-dark-ages. htm.

5. Boogieman | Define Boogieman at Dictionary.com dictionary.com/ browse/boogieman.

6. Political Correctness – See Part I, #4, #5 in Notes.

7. Bellwether | Definition of Bellwether by Merriam-Webster merriam-webster.com/dictionary/bellwether.

8. Market Correction Definition and Example | InvestingAnswers investinganswers.com/financial-dictionary/...market/market-correction-2491.

9. Referendum | definition in the Cambridge Dictionary dictionary.cambridge.org/us/dictionary/English/referendum.

10. Atrocity – See Chapter 4, #4 in Glossary Notes.

11. Concrete – See Chapter 12, #13 in Notes.

12. Trilogy of Understanding – I devised this term. See Chapter 14 in Glossary.

Chapter 16

1. Wolf, Byron Z. Could Sanders have won primary that wasn't 'rigged'? – CNNPolitics 4 November 2017. cnn.com/2017/11/04/politics/bernie-sanders-2016-election.../index.html.

2. Binary | Definition of Binary by Merriam-Webster merriam-webster.com/dictionary/binary.

Chapter 17

No notes in this section.

Chapter 18

1. Pop/Political Culture – I devised this term. See Chapter 4 in Glossary.

2. Political Psychosis – See Chapter 13 in Glossary.

3. "Trump" Market Correction – See Chapters 15 and 18 in Glossary.

4. Ergo – Google Chrome. Dictionary.

Afterword

1. Stylings – See Chapter 1, #2 in Glossary Notes.

2. Unalienable Rights – See Chapter 2, #5 in Notes.

3. Cognitive Dissonance – See Chapter 6, #8 in Notes.

4. Concrete Thinking – See Chapter 12, #13 in Notes.

5. Projective Identification – See Chapter 12, #11 in Notes.

Index

www.ingramcontent.com/pod-product-compliance
Lightning Source LLC
Chambersburg PA
CBHW060316030426
42336CB00011B/1077